Small Acts

Thoughts on the politics of black cultures

Paul Gilroy

Library of Congress Catalog Card Number 93-84757

A CIP record for this book can be obtained from the
British Library on request

The right of Paul Gilroy to be identified as author of this
work has been asserted by him in accordance with the
Copyright, Designs and Patents Act 1988

First published in 1993 by
Serpent's Tail, 4 Blackstock Mews, London N4, and
401 West Broadway #1, New York, NY 10012

Reprinted 2005

Typeset in 10½ on 14pt Sabon by Method Limited,
Epping, Essex
Printed in Finland by Werner Söderström Oy

Printed & Bound by Digisource (GB) Ltd
Livingston, Scotland, UK.
Reprinted 2005

Paul Gilroy is senior lecturer in sociology at Goldsmiths' College, London University. He has taught at South Bank Polytechnic and the University of Essex and held a visiting professorship at Yale. He is the author of *There Ain't No Black in the Union Jack* and *The Black Atlantic* and co-author of *The Empire Strikes Back*.

Contents

Introduction

This is a difficult moment for the black cultures of the Western world and for their critics, wherever they are located in the African diaspora. In England as elsewhere, the effortless certainties that guided the creation and the use of dissident black cultures in earlier times have evaporated in stressful new historical conditions for which no precedents exist. The fundamental, time-worn assumption of homogenous and unchanging black communities whose political and economic interests were readily knowable and easily transferred from everyday life into their expressive cultures has, for example, proved to be a fantasy. To make matters worse, the ideal of racial purity, the appeal of phenotypical symmetry and the comfort of cultural sameness have never been more highly prized as attributes of black social life than they are today. However, lived profane differences within Britain's black communities have stubbornly refused to disappear under the pressure from this racial narcissism. They have coexisted uncomfortably with the demand for purity and sameness, challenging it and answering its over-simple pictures of an unstable world in which no single way of living, thinking and being black is able to claim automatic priority over all the others. The existence of a multiplicity of black tones and styles has created new political tensions and a debate over the possibility and desirability of rules that could govern the production of black art and culture. Intra-racial differences have been compounded and amplified as familiar but deeply repressed divisions based on class, ideology and money; language and locality have been supplemented by intense and irrepressible antagonisms arising from sexuality, gender and generation. These social divisions inside the racial kin group are no longer seen as secondary or trivial. Both those who want to celebrate this pluralization of black identities and those who oppose it and want to reinstate an innocent idea of simple racial essences have had to recognize their importance. All through the summer of 1992 the cheerful, throaty refrain of 'Boom bye bye ina de batty man head' conveyed just how important indexing these differences had become for the formation of an arrogant racial absolutism that encompassed callous homophobia but moved far beyond it in pursuit of a militarized machismo that could make everybody certain about blackness once again and then command their allegiance. The idea of a common, invariant racial identity capable of linking divergent black experiences across different spaces and times has been fatally undermined. The increasingly desperate assertions of homogeneity that flow out of black vernacular culture can neither conceal nor answer this transformation. Homogeneity can signify unity but unity need not require homogeneity. Religious and political movements have emerged which regiment and synchronize the bodies of their black affiliates with uniforms and mass rituals. Unlike the Garvey movement which preceded them, these groups are trying to create and harness a sense of sameness that does not exist prior to their attempts to manufacture it. Their increasingly popular activities are a response to a situation where neither the effects of white supremacy nor the historic momentum of subaltern racial identities marked by slavery and colonialism can be relied upon to establish the feelings of connectedness that have been identified as a precondition for racial survival.

These changes in the black communities' self-understanding affect the formation, reproduction, dissemination and use of their expressive cultures in quite fundamental ways. People who want to write analytically about black cultures will have to learn to cope with them. This is a difficult process. The position of black cultural critics is rendered still more uncomfortable because, in England at least, the space in which serious public discussion of the politics of black cultural production can take place has dwindled. This shrinkage is another symptom of a new condition in which the old commitment to debate and discussion as a means to strengthen the culture is being replaced by a mood that reduces race politics to little more than a form of communal therapy and makes critical judgements on black culture impossible to articulate. In this climate, to be critical or analytical is often perceived to be an act of betrayal. Where these accusations are made, the essential black identity which must be safeguarded at all costs turns out to be a surprisingly brittle construction. The therapeutic moment is an important and maybe necessary one in the reproduction of political movements and oppositional subjectivities but we are paying a high price for accepting its creeping domination of our political culture. A generation insulated from self-activity by the economic and political cushion of local state anti-racism has become timid. Unable to see outside the confines of its own experience of subordination it has discovered pleasure in the performance of absolute identity to which the theatre of powerlessness plays host.

Further difficulties have arisen because the precious, fragile spaces that remain are regularly occupied by conflict between two assertive groups which are engaged in vicious battles that almost conceal their symbiotic interdependency. The first tendency is composed of people who have an essentially commercial orientation towards black cultures. This takes various forms but the basic interest in the marketing and commodification of objects and processes that resist transmutation into passive saleable items regularly requires the traffickers in black culture to deny that their chosen commodity has any political dimensions at all. This is done in order that it can be sold more easily. Black cultures can be marketed to blacks in this bland, anodyne form but the anti-political approach is even stronger where the signs of blackness have been specially packaged in order to cross over to white consumers, many of whom take pleasure in the transgression and dangerousness which these once-forbidden commodities express, without discovering a similar enthusiasm for either the company of real live black people or the history of their struggles against slavery, for citizenship and towards personal and social autonomy. In filleted form, black culture can also be annexed in order to sell other kinds of commodities. The sampled beat from James Brown's 'Funky Drummer' adds its special allure to advertisements for upscale German cars, while commercial radio stations that started out as pirates and were fuelled by the disenchantment born of black exclusion from the public sphere now deploy the minimal sounds of blackness to construct an audience that they can sell to their advertisers.

Opposition to the marketers and merchandisers has been dominated by an altogether different position. This proceeds from a belief that black culture is nothing but its politics. The anti-political manoeuvres of the first group and the associated desire to make commercial success the exclusive arbiter of cultural value is rightly attacked. However, the alternative understanding of political processes to which this group subscribes is disappointingly and frustratingly narrow. Cultural politics gets confined to the tasks of producing and defending racial particularity and identity as well as the exhilarating job of disciplining anyone who is either bold or stupid enough to disagree with the occultist formulations that arise in an antique drama of racial metaphysics. Surprisingly, there is considerable traffic on the

road between these two encampments. Part of the novelty of the
present situation is conveyed by an exceptional degree of ideological fluidity which enables the various producers, sellers and
users of black culture to exchange one 'pragmatic' outlook for
another equally contingent one without even the sanction of
shame. Squeezed between these interchangeable options is a
third formation. It is linked at one end to what might be called
the black arts movement and at the other to a different set of
commercial strategies premised on the idea that unfashionable
commitments to the healing and liberating power of black culture must be retained. From Sonya Boyce and Keith Piper to
Rebel MC's Tribal Base via Isaac Julien and Jazzie B., the actions
of this diverse group are linked by the thin threads of its common insistence on accountability and open-ended enthusiasm
for spurning the easy, lazy options that reduce race politics to the
simple binary code of black and white.

The greatly expanded market for black cultures sets the standards for their value. Its authority is unchallenged and the effec-
tive privatization of black cultures proceeds as the passive
consumption of received images begins to dominate the older
strategies for active use of culture that derived from slavery and
continue to work best with oppositional forms that are based on
sound and music rather than text and image. Music, which was
the centre of black vernacular culture for such a long time, has
acquired a new place and a new significance. It is no longer the
hermeneutic key to a whole medley of expressive practices and is
infrequently appreciated for itself or for its capacity to express
the inexpressible and communicate the effects of a history of
barbarity that exhausts the resources of language. Its non-repre-
sentational qualities are being pressed into service to do an
uncomplicated representational job. They are burdened with the
task of conjuring up a utopia of racial authenticity that is everywhere denied but still sought nonetheless. This new role for

music as a cipher for authenticity has developed hand in hand with a technological revolution in musical production. The control of multinational corporations has been loosened and music-making and distribution have become less capital- and labour-intensive, while public musical performances are becoming more and more expensive to produce. The most depressing aspect of this historical shift is the process of radical de-skilling which has destroyed the magical cultural authority of instrumentalists. But the revolution of digital technology is not a wholly negative development: the destructive impact of de-skilling must be seen in relation to its clear implications for the demystification and democratization of the culture. Producing music without an element of performance to mediate its creation and its social use feeds the privatization of cultural production and can isolate the music-makers from the social exchanges and disciplines of the alternative public spheres which have nurtured black musical sub-cultures for so long. The Bomb Squad's Hank Shocklee has warned that live performances may soon be a thing of the past and asks what the consequences of this change will be for the evolving tradition of black music-making. However defiant and insubordinate its muses are, most of the music produced in the bedroom on samplers and drum machines lacks the moral authority that once grew from the informal negotiations between performers and crowds. Antiphony is not structured into it from its inception. Indeed, this new black music is increasingly not produced at all but playfully and creatively recycled from a standard lexicon of break beats and other sampled sounds.

It is interesting that music has come to signify authenticity at the very moment when it has evolved into new styles that are inescapably hybrid and multiplex in character. Hip-hop was not an ethnically pure or particular African-American product but rather the mutant result of fusion and intermixture with

Caribbean cultures from Jamaica and Puerto Rico. Its outernational and intercultural origins are effectively concealed by powerful ethnocentric accounts of its history that see it merely as a direct descendant of jazz, soul and blues. Instead, the circulation and mutation of black musics provide a powerful illustration of how the untidy patterns of differentiation and sameness to which a diaspora gives rise might yield a novel notion of tradition as the medium for exchange and creative development rather than invariant repetition.

Sexuality and gender identity are the other privileged media that express the evasive but highly prized quality of racial authenticity. Their growing power in configuring contemporary notions of blackness raises once again the critical issue of how the complex dynamics of race and gender come together. In a situation where racial identity appears suddenly impossible to know reliably or maintain with ease, the naturalness of gender can supply the modality in which race is lived and symbolized. This may explain why so much black vernacular art treats extensively on these subjects, at times even suggesting that the intensity with which gender identity is held and gender conflicts are experienced is a consequence of racial difference. The popularity of slackness and the more misogynist forms of hip-hop can be used to support this diagnosis. The chief effect of this unhappy situation is that today's crisis of black social life is routinely represented as a crisis of masculinity alone. The integrity of the race is defined primarily as the integrity of its menfolk and secondarily through the patriarchally ordered nature of the families over which they would proudly and justly preside if white supremacy did not intervene and create catastrophe. This position reached its fullest expression so far in Shaharazad Ali's best-selling book *The Black Man's Guide to Understanding the Black Woman* but it is also expressed in widespread arguments for defensive blackonly schooling and other forms of institutional segregation. It has disastrous consequences for black women who are required to submit to the forms of family life that are supposedly capable of restoring a maleness which has been damaged by the corrosive effects of white power and reproducing it in more durable and ethnically appropriate forms. It is also disastrous for black men, who are invited to inhabit a toughened mode of masculinity which has been racially endorsed and invested with the special glamour of authenticity. This is an austere, Spartan masculinity that constructs its patriarchal techniques from blending a blunt authoritarianism with the shape-shifting cunning of the black hustler. Its central characteristic is that it has been stripped of all tenderness, for expressions of tenderness are now dismissed as signs of weakness, just as ruthlessness and violence are exalted over love. As with so many of the seductive fruits of voguish Africentrism, the public sphere seems to have been entirely abandoned. The inward, implosive direction of this kind of consciousness is shown by progressive reductions in the symbolic area over which power is exercised. This intimate space is reduced first to the household, then to the body and its clothing and finally to the process of renaming oneself. It is not that these areas are unimportant, but rather that they should not be the only ones to define the scope and the hopes of black political culture.

The word 'crisis' has been terribly over-used in the rhetorics of black political culture and cultural politics. However, thinking about crisis as a combination of danger and opportunity is inescapable if we are to locate and comprehend both the forms of jeopardy experienced by blacks in the overdeveloped countries and the responses that black cultures make to these conditions. This profound crisis is not something that these essays can stand outside and I hope that a sense of its dimensions emerges from reading them. A preliminary discussion of it may be useful, if only to guide the reader towards my understanding of its general symptoms and their fragmentary inscription in the texts that follow.

I see the effects of this multidimensional crisis as layered, onion-like, around the core of black cultural expressions that these pieces explore. It is a lived crisis as well as a system crisis. Most fundamentally, it is a crisis that demonstrates how closely bound up the fate of blacks is with the fortunes of the overdeveloped world, even where we dissent from its logics and its hopes. Blacks were bound to the deepest structures of Euro-American modernity by slavery. In the period since then the desperate manner in which we have sometimes retreated from it into the shell of an imagined anti-modern Africanity betrays us. Even our gestures of disaffiliation can unwittingly confirm just how Western and modern we are. The understanding of 'race' that we use almost without thinking, the ideas of nationality and culture with which we support it and the fundamental aspiration to freedom with which we orient our actions all derive from a history of ideas that has been integral to modern racial typology and white supremacy. This is a history, furthermore, in which the forces of civilization and progress have been entirely complicit with the sustained practice of racial terror. Our debts to that history are so extensive that debating the ultimate utility of the master's tools in dismantling the master's house is pointless – merely gestural. Even if we spurn his toolkit, the plans we need in order to complete the job of demolition without injuring ourselves in the process were produced according to his assumptions. We built the house, but according to his design. Our labour means that we have invested something of ourselves in its structure and that simple fact gives us a claim to ownership that we should not renounce too lightly. Perhaps the binary notion of two ideal, warring racial selves presupposed by this type of argument is one of the worst tricks that the master's traditions of thought can play upon those who would like to be free.

The vision of crisis as danger and opportunity, lived and systematic, can also give due weight to the macro-structural and economic conditions that shape the locations in which black creativity develops. It is hard to talk about these factors while treating black expressive culture autonomously and with the reverence and respect that its significance as a global political resource demands. However, these structural factors are important because they affect the political options that mediate our understanding of and responses to de-industrialization and the distinctive patterns of authoritarian government that have accompanied it. The black expressive cultures of the last decade or so communicate a sense of these structural constraints very powerfully. I do not want to minimize those aspects of this perilous predicament that are economic and systematic or exist beyond the scope of any individual grasp. However, the emphasis which emerges in the pieces that follow this introduction argues for a different sense of priorities. This is based not on appreciating the extent of political and economic constraints on black creativity but on seeking to maximize a sense of the opportunities for democratic, oppositional agency that can exist even in the most restricted circumstances.

One of the strongest themes to appear within contemporary black vernacular culture is the idea that there are limits to what we can blame on the leviathan of white supremacy. This idea, expressed so cogently in collective musical projects from The Stop The Violence Movement, The West Coast Rap All Stars and H.E.A.L. in the United States and B.R.O.T.H.E.R., Britain's lone voice against drug-induced fratricide, machismo and hopelessness, says that blacks should seek to take responsibility for the self-destructive features of our social behaviour and pay attention to the hurt that we cause each other as well as the injuries that a racially stratified world inflicts upon us. It says, in other words, that we must pay attention to both inside and outside

aspects of our experiences of subordination if we are to comprehend it properly. This important stance is closely associated with
another valuable insight, namely that there is far more to the
content of black social and cultural life than the effects of racism
alone. These reflexive positions are sometimes associated with a
move towards the decidedly Victorian notions of individualism
and racial uplift that found favour in the atmosphere created by
Mrs Thatcher's brand of racially coded, populist and nationalist
conservatism. The idea that individual development, strength
and energy are all that is necessary for the social progress of the
racial community as a whole has, for example, provided a ratio-
nale for the expansion of black business interests and economic
strategies towards self-reliance. These initiatives are limited in a
country where the black population is so small and diverse but
they have seemed genuinely to have the well-being of the black
communities at heart. This link with conservatism has been
important in changing the terms of black political discourse and
may be an ironic expression of the growing maturity of black
political responses, now happily detached from any automatic
loyalty to the party that passed the Race Relations Acts long ago.

Yet this tie to a conservative political outlook is not an
inevitable or irresistible feature, nor is it the result of paying
closer attention to areas of individual and social responsibility
that have been neglected in the past. The reflexive, self-critical
spirit that guides it can be readily uncoupled from its conservative expressions and used to usher in a different perspective on
self and sociality in which black communities are able, in spite of
the pressures that flow from their historical and contemporary
victimization, to take a measure of responsibility for changing
their situation. This may also mean trading in the moral benefits
of victim status for something more challenging and more radical – a sense of ourselves as agents in the endless struggle
towards our own emancipation. It bears repetition that the

structural pressures bearing down on black communities from the outside are complemented and amplified by intra-racial antagonisms which make those communities appear to be more internally divided than ever. Poverty, drug abuse, violence and black-on-black crime are only the most obvious contributory factors here. They create and index a situation where the forms of black solidarity that were constructed during the era of black power and pride simply cannot be assumed to operate any longer, where brotherhood and sisterhood should not be assumed to exist but are waiting to be re-created.

The inherent mutuality of Ethiopianism and pan-Africanism and the communitarian elements of Rastafari livity have not been entirely replaced by the brutal, competitive spirit celebrated so elaborately and enthusiastically in popular cultural phenomena like Victor Headley's novel *Yardie* and affirmed repeatedly in many other vernacular exaltations of raggamuffin ruthlessness. The cultural tide has turned decisively against ideas of racial kinship produced in the 1960s to do a particular job and which appear now as naive, outdated and sentimental. This has happened at the same time that the iconography and style of these older black movements have been recycled and cannibalized. Often it is employed as a device that adds ill-deserved ethical weight and moral legitimacy to contemporary opportunism and cynicism.

The social memory of the black movements of the 1960s is important for other reasons too. Its creative appropriation marks black Britain's sharp turn away from the Caribbean as its major source of inspiration. Black political culture in this country now looks to African-American history for guidance, pleasure and raw material for its own distinct definitions of blackness. The appeal of the heroic figure of Malcolm X has been central to this development. It expresses not just the collapse of the black churches' spiritual authority but a yearning for forms of redemptive and visionary leadership that have never been a feature of black political culture in Britain. It represents the latest triumph of outer-national and intercultural political forms that make their local equivalents, still bolted to the decaying chassis of a nineteenth-century nation-state, look tame, redundant and outmoded by comparison. The crucial role that reading Malcolm's autobiography has played in disseminating his narrative of self-creation and transformation is one reason that this focused longing is unlikely to be completely recuperated into an empty, depthless politics of style.

The recovery of Malcolm X can be readily interpreted as a restoration of the black manhood that white supremacy denies but it is a contradictory process in which an unusual and potent mixture of due reverence and psychosexual identification needs to be explained rather than concealed. Of course, the resurgence of interest in Malcolm guarantees nothing about the progressive character or radical direction of black politics in the future. Part of Malcolm's appeal is the openness of his narrative. This allows him to appear in myriad guises: as an orthodox member of the Nation of Islam, as a prototype for Minister Farrakhan or as a fledgling revolutionary socialist. We must try to make sense of the apparently limitless post-modern plasticity of Malcolm. His most enduring and powerful incarnation seems to be as a patriarchal sign in the family romance that black political history has become. Like Malcolm's own story of transformation and redemptive change, the capacity to remake and mould his memory into a variety of contradictory but equally valid shapes underlines the impossibility of seeing racial identity in mechanistically essentialist terms. Loving Malcolm is more appropriately interpreted as a desire to set the historical memory of black struggles loose in a world where memory and historicity have been subordinated to a relentless contemporaneity. Apart from anything else, his life represents the possibility of a link between blacks in the overdeveloped countries and the substantive political concerns arising not from an ideal mythical Africa symbolized by the greatness of its past and anterior civilization, but from the medical, ecological and economic problems of Africa's present. His living memory and the power of his image have created an important opportunity to find new sets of racial tactics in circumstances where black nationalism and the economistic leftism against which it was so often defined have nothing left to offer.

The essays below develop many of the ideas sketched in this introduction. I hope they make it clear that the totalizing schemes of macro-political narrative are not to my taste. However, there is no suggestion that a political language based on racial identification should be abandoned. It may be insufficient but it remains necessary in a world where racisms continue to proliferate and flourish. Refusing race as a critical category would not do anything to undermine or interrupt these racisms, many of which can operate quite effectively without resort to it. Instead, I suggest that we strive to find a different path from the familiar ones that lead respectively to the resoluteness of therapeutic essentialism and the squeamishness of anti-essentialisms which are complacent about the continuing effects of racism. It might be more fruitful to explore the dynamics of an anti-essentialism that did not trade in essentialist configurations of racial selves and racial cultures, an anti-essentialism that emphasized the issue of accountability in its practical commitment to democracy and set the cultivation of affinity alongside the mechanics of identity. Perhaps this anti-essentialism could approach the everyday world, mindful of its comprehensive asymmetry, and work to locate a different fragmentary beauty amidst the irreducible chaos of racial antagonisms. Its motto would be that understanding the radical contingency of racial identities does not diminish their power.

In tune with these hopes, I want these essays to convey a way of interpreting black cultural forms politically without reducing them to their politics alone. I have tried to preserve the tension between broadly defined political imperatives and the non-negotiable autonomy of cultural expression even while acknowledging the distinctive ways that black cultural practice brings these two aspects of social life together and often revels in their connectedness. Many of the judgements in these pieces are contentious and their theoretical aspects remain doggedly engaged in a practical mode. Whether they inspire or enrage, I would only ask that people try to read them as a plea to be more imaginative and more speculative in our readings of black culture. Heterodox opinions justify themselves not because they are correct or conclusive, but because we need to be able to ask questions without knowing where answering them will lead. I hope that *Small Acts* deploys elements of utopian and politicized postmodernism against the spurious certainties of racial realism. The resort to ethnic absolutism can only be a source of weakness in the long run. It is already a source of inertia and confusion.

PART ONE

Black and English:
a lived contradiction

1 One nation under a groove

... how much is here embraced by the term culture. It includes all the characteristic activities and interests of a people: Derby Day, Henley Regatta, Cowes, the twelfth of August, a cup final, the dog races, the pin table, the dart board, Wensleydale cheese, boiled cabbage cut into sections, beetroot in vinegar, nineteenth century Gothic churches and the music of Elgar.

T. S. Eliot

While there is some community of interest called Britain and common institutions and historical experiences called British, and indeed a nationality on a passport called British, it is not an identity which is self contained . . . Britain is a state rather than a nation. The British state imposed upon the English, Scottish, Welsh and part of the Irish peoples and then imposed world wide, is an inherently imperial and colonial concept at home and abroad. The British state cannot and should not be an object of affection, save for those who want to live in a form of authoritarian dependency.

Dafydd Elis Thomas

This chapter was originally written for the anthology *Anatomy of Racism*, edited by David Theo Goldberg and published by University of Minnesota Press (1990).

Studying the politics of 'race'[1] necessitates tracing at least two separate yet intertwined threads of history. The first involves mapping the changing contours of racist ideologies, the semantic fields in which they operate, their special rhetoric and their internal fractures as well as their continuities. The second centres on the history of social groups, both dominant and subordinate, which recognize themselves in terms of race and act accordingly. Neither of these histories is reducible to the other and they reciprocate in a complex manner over time, bringing together the myths of descent with the management of conquest and the negotiation of consent.

The groups we learn to know as races are not, of course, formed simply and exclusively by the power of racial discourses. The intimate association between ideas about race and the employment of unfree labour in plantation slavery, 'debt peonage', apartheid or the coercive use of migrant labour should be a constant warning against conceptualizing racial ideologies as if they are wholly autonomous. Race may provide literary critics, with 'the ultimate trope of difference' but the brain-teasing perplexities of theorizing about race cannot be allowed to obscure the fact that the play of difference in which racial taxonomy appears has extra-discursive referents. At different times, economic, political and cultural factors all play a determining role in shaping the character of races. The power of race politics can be used as a general argument for realist conceptions of ideology which emphasize referential conceptions of meaning and defend a problematic of relative or partial autonomy.[2]

Races are not, then, simple expressions of either biological or cultural sameness. They are imagined – socially and politically constructed – and the contingent processes from which they emerge may be tied to equally uneven patterns of class formation to which they, in turn, contribute. Thus ideas about race may articulate political and economic relations in a particular society which go beyond the distinct experiences or interests of racial groups to symbolize wider identities and conflicts. Discussion of racial domination cannot therefore be falsely separated from wider considerations of social sovereignty such as the conflict between men and women, the antagonism between capital and labour or the manner in which modes of production develop and combine. Nor can the complexities of racial politics be reduced to the effect of these other relations. Dealing with these issues in their specificity and in their articulation with other relations and practices constitutes a profound and urgent theoretical and political challenge. It requires a theory of racisms which does not depend on an essentialist theory of races themselves.

These methodological observations help to negotiate a critical distance from positivist and productivist Marxian and neo-Marxian approaches which risk the reduction of 'race' to a mystical conception of class as well as those which have buried the specific qualities of racism in the difficulties surrounding the analysis of ideology in general. Pursuing a radical analysis of race and racism within the broad framework that historical materialism supplies, requires a frank and open acknowledgement of its limitations. Yet Marxism understood in Richard Wright's phrase as a 'transitory makeshift pending a more accurate diagnosis'[3] can provide some valuable points of departure. If the capacity of race and racism to slide between the realm of 'phenomenal forms' and the world of 'real relations' means that they have baffled and perplexed Marxian orthodoxy,[4] there is much to learn from the radically historical approach which has emerged from some of the more sophisticated applications of Marx's insights. Working from an explicitly Marxian perspective, Stuart Hall puts it like this:

> Racism is always historically specific. Though it may draw on the cultural traces deposited by previous historical phases, it

> always takes on specific forms. It arises out of present – not
> past – conditions, its effects are specific to the present
> organisation of society, to the present unfolding of its
> dynamic political and cultural processes – not simply to its
> repressed past.[5]

This important observation points squarely at the plurality of
forms in which racism has developed, not simply between societies but within them also. It underlines the idea that there is no
racism in general and consequently there can be no general theory of race relations or race and politics. More importantly, a
perspective which emphasizes the need to deal with racisms
rather than a single ahistorical racism also implicitly attacks the
fashionable over-identification of race and ethnicity with tradition, allowing instead the opportunity to develop a view of contemporary racisms as responses to the flux of modernity itself.[6]

This perspective places severe limitations on analysis of particular local racisms. It demands that the development of racist
discourses must be periodized very carefully and that the fluidity
and inherent instability of racial categories is constantly appreciated. With these qualifications in mind, I want to examine some
aspects of recent race politics in Britain: by looking first at the
particular contemporary forms of racist discourse, and second,
at the distinctive political outlook articulated by the expressive
cultures of England's black settlers.

The starting point for this inquiry must be an acknowledgement of Britain's post-colonial decline and crisis. Although this
crisis originates in the economic sphere,[7] it has a variety of features – economic, political, ideological and cultural. They are
not wholly discrete and although they are definitely discontinuous, they are experienced as a complex unity of many unsyn-
chronized determinations. How then is this unity constructed? I
want to suggest that ideas about 'race' which are produced by a

new and historically specific form of racism play a primary role in securing it. This crisis is thus *lived* through a sense of 'race'. A volatile populist racism has become an obvious political feature of this crisis. But racism is more than simply an increasingly important component of a morbid political culture. It has also become part of how the different elements of this protracted 'organic' crisis have become articulated together.[8]

The centrality of racism to this crisis does not, however, mean that the word 'race' is on everybody's lips. It bears repetition that racism changes and varies historically. It is essential to remember that we are not talking about racism in general, but British crisis racism in particular. One of the ways in which this form or variety of racism is specific is that it frequently operates without any overt reference to either 'race' itself or the biological notions of difference which still give the term its common-sense meaning. Before the rise of modern scientific racism in the nineteenth-century, the term 'race' did duty for the term 'culture'.[9] No surprise then, that in its post-war retreat from fascism the term has once again acquired an explicitly cultural rather than a biological inflection.

The stress and turbulence of crisis have induced Britons to clarify their national identity by asking themselves a question first posed by Enoch Powell: 'What kind of people are we?' Their self-scrutiny has prompted a fascination with primary, ascribed identities which is manifested in an increasingly decadent preoccupation with the metaphysics of national belonging. Examining contemporary British ideas about race and their relationship to notions of nationhood and national belonging in particular, can therefore tell us something about the crisis as a whole.

It would appear that the uncertainty which the crisis has created requires that lines of inclusion and exclusion which mark out the national community are redrawn. Britons are invited to put on their tin hats and climb back down into their World War II air-raid shelters. There, they can be comforted by the rustic glow of the homogenous national culture that has been steadily diluted by black settlement in the post-war years. That unsullied culture can be mystically reconstituted, particularly amidst national adversity when distinctively British qualities supposedly emerge with the greatest force and clarity. The analogy of war is extensively employed, not just in attempts to represent black immigration and settlement as the encroachment of aliens but around the politics of crime and domestic political dissent. Industrial militants and black settlers have come to share the designation 'the enemy within'. In 1982, real war off the coast of Argentina provided, in the words of one New Right ideologue, an opportunity for the nation to discover 'what truly turns it on'. From this perspective, which has provided a cornerstone for popular, common-sense racism, blacks, trapped by the biology of their skin shade into a form of symbolic treason, are excluded from the national community because their cultures have obstructed the acquisition of that special hallmark of a true patriotism: the willingness to lay down one's life for one's country.

The culturalism of the new racism has gone hand in hand with a definition of race as a matter of difference rather than a question of hierarchy. In another context, Fanon refers to a similar shift as a progression from vulgar to cultural racism.[10] The same process is clearly seen in the cultural focus which marked the inauguration of the apartheid system in 1948.

Culture is conceived along ethnically absolute lines, not as something intrinsically fluid, changing, unstable and dynamic, but as a fixed property of social groups rather than a relational field in which they encounter one another and live out social, historical relationships. When culture is brought into contact with 'race' it is transformed into a pseudo-biological property of communal life.

Thus England's black settlers are forever locked in the bastard culture of their enslaved ancestors, unable to break out into the 'mainstream' alternative. Their presence in the ancient territory of the 'island race' becomes a problem precisely because of their difference and distance from the standards of civilized behaviour which are second nature to authentic (white) Britons. The most vocal ideologists of the English New Right[11] – Powell himself, John Casey and Ray Honeyford – stress not only that they are not racists but that they have no sense whatever of the innate superiority of whites or the congenital inferiority of blacks. They profess allegiance to the nation rather than the race and identify the problems of contemporary black settlement in terms of cultural conflict between the same groups which were once misrecognized as biologically distinct races. This cultural sense of 'race' has posed key problems for anti-racist strategy and tactics.

As the distance from crude biologism has increased, the question of law has become more important as a marker for the cultural processes involved. English law is presented as the summit of the national civilization, the pinnacle of Britain's historic achievements. An unwritten constitution distils the finest qualities of the national community and enshrines them in an historic compact to which blacks are unable to adhere. Black violations of the law supply the final proof of their incompatibility with Britain. Their 'illegal immigration' and a propensity to street crime confirm their alien status. These specific forms of lawbreaking are, as I have shown elsewhere, gradually defined as a cultural attribute of the black population as a whole.

One significant continuity with the colonial setting can be identified in the way that the most potent symbols of the national culture are not merely racialized but gendered too. Once-proud Britannia has, like her declining nation, fallen on hard times. A resurgent nativist politics has recast her as an aged white woman. Initially violated by Powell's demons, the 'wide-grinning piccaninnies' who chase her through the streets chanting 'racial-ist', she is, with the onset of their adolescence, terrorized by them again when they turn to more financially remunerative forms of harassment like 'mugging'. The predatory figure of the black rapist also makes an appearance here, demonstrating the failure of the civilizing process and the resistance of black culture to its evangelical imperatives.[12] For a long while, the question of black criminality provided the principal means to underscore the *cultural* concerns of this new racism. Its dominance helped to locate precisely where the new racism began – in the bloody nightmare of the old woman pursued through the streets by black children. However, crime has been displaced recently at the centre of race politics by another issue which points equally effectively to the supposed incompatibility of different cultures sealed off from one another forever along ethnic lines. This too uses images of the black child to make its point. It seems that the cultural sins of the immigrant fathers will be visited on their British-born children. Where once it was the mean streets of the decaying inner city which hosted the most fearsome encounter between white Britons and their most improbable and intimidating other – black youth – now it is the classrooms and staffrooms of the nation's inner-city schools which frame the same conflict and provide the most potent terms with which to make sense of racial difference.

The recent publication of *Anti-racism: An Assault on Education and Value*[13] confirmed the fact that the school has become the principal element in the ideology with which the English New Right have sought to attack anti-racism. It is essen-tial to understand *why* their burgeoning anti-anti-racism has shifted the emphasis from crime to education. Although it poses a range of different strategic difficulties, the change may be less significant than it may first appear. Schools are defined by the right as repositories of the authentic national culture which they transmit between generations. They mediate the relation of the national community to its youthful future citizens. Decaying school buildings provide a ready image for the nation in microcosm. The hard-won changes which anti-racists and multiculturalists have wrought on the curriculum come to exemplify the debasement of all genuine British culture. Anti-racist initiatives that supposedly denigrate educational standards are identified as an assault on the 'traditional virtues' of British education. This cultural conflict is a means through which the dynamics of power are transposed, and whites become a voiceless ethnic minority oppressed by the anti-racist policies of totalitarian Labour local authorities. In the same ideological movement, the racists are redefined as the blacks and their allies, and Mr Honeyford becomes a tenacious defender of freedom who is invited in to the inner sanctums of government as a consultant.

If the importance of culture rather than biology is the first quality which marks this form of racism as something different and new, the special ties it discovers between race, culture and nation provide further evidence of its novelty. The expansive ideology of the Commonwealth and the imperial family of nations bonded in common citizenship has given way to a more parochial and embittered perspective which sees culture in neat and tidy national formations. The family remains a key motif but the multiracial family of nations has been displaced by the racially homogeneous nation of families. The nation is composed of even, symmetrical family units which, like Mr Honeyford's beleaguered inner-city school, transmit folk traditions between generations. The emphasis on culture allows nation and race to fuse. Nationalism and racism become so closely identified that to speak of the nation is to speak automatically in racially exclusive terms. Blackness and Englishness are constructed as incompatible, mutually exclusive identities. To speak of the British or English people is to speak of the *white*

people. Brief consideration of the British general election of summer 1987 allows us to see these themes and conflicts played out
with a special clarity. The theme of patriotism was well to the
fore and a tussle over the national flag was a major feature of the
campaign. The Labour Party pleaded for Britain to heal its deep
internal divisions and become 'one nation again' while the
Conservatives underlined their success in 'putting the Great back
into Britain' by urging the electorate not to let the socialists take
this crucial adjective out again. Significantly, this language made
no overt reference to 'race' but it acquired racial referents.
Everyone knows what is at stake when patriotism and deference
to the law are being spoken about. The seamless manner in
which the themes of race, culture and nation came together was
conveyed by a racist leaflet issued in the North London constituency of Bernie Grant, a black Labour candidate who had
achieved national prominence in the aftermath of the 1985 riots
as an apologist for the rioters. It was illustrated by a picture of
his head grafted onto the hairy body of a gorilla. It read:

> Swing along with Bernie it's the very natural thing
> He's been doing it for centuries and now he thinks he's king
> He's got a little empire and he doesn't give a jot
> But then the British are a bloody tolerant lot
> They'll let him swing and holler hetero – Homo – Gay
> And then just up and shoot him in the good old British way

These lines signify a powerful appropriation of the rights and
liberties of the free-born Briton, once so beloved of the English
New Left. The rhyme's historical references demonstrate how
completely blackness and Britishness have been made into mutually exclusive categories, incompatible identities. It would appear
that the problems which Bernie represents are most clearly visible
against the patterned backdrop of the Union Jack. The picture of

him as a gorilla is necessary on the leaflet because its words make no overt mention of his inferior biology. The crime for which he may be justifiably lynched is a form of treason, not the transgression involved in mere racial inferiority. The poem knits together images invoking empire, sovereignty and sexuality (an allusion to the local council's progressive policy on lesbian and gay rights), with its exhortation to violence. There is nothing about this combination of themes which marks it out as the exclusive preserve of the right. The leaflet provides a striking example of how the racism which ties national cultures to ethnic essences, which sees custom, law and constitution, schools and courts of justice beset by corrosive alien forces, has moved beyond the grasp of the old left/right distinction. The populist character of the new racism is crucial. It works across the lines of formal politics as well as within them. It can link together disparate and antagonistic groups, leading them to discover the morbid pleasures of seeing themselves as 'one nation', inviting them to draw comfort from a mythic sense of past[14] as it is reconstructed as historical memory in the present.

As a political issue, concern with the erosion of the national culture is perhaps spontaneously identified with the self-consciously conservative postures of the right. The emphasis on crime and the law, which identified the early stages of the new cultural racism, also emerged from that quarter. However, many of the same ideas about what race, nation and culture mean and how they fit together are held more broadly. Sections of the left have recently stressed the issues of crime and patriotism without regard for any of their racial connotations. More significantly and ironically, some vocal factions inside the black communities have also sought to emphasize the cultural incompatibility of Afro-Caribbean and Asian settlers with Britain and Britishness. Ultra-right, new left and black nationalists can accept variations of the idea that Britain may be a multiracial society but is not yet and may never be a multiracial nation.

The convergence between the left and right over what race means in contemporary Britain can be illustrated by looking at Raymond Williams's brief discussion of race in *Towards 2000*.[15] In this passage, Williams not only proved himself unable to address the issue of racism, he unwittingly echoed Powell in arguing that there was far more to authentic 'lived and formed' national identity than the rights conferred by the 'alienated superficialities' of formal citizenship. For blacks denied access to meaningful citizenship by the operation of a 'grandfather clause', these legal rights are rather more than superficial. Indeed, they have constituted the substance of a protracted political conflict with which Williams is clearly unfamiliar. I am not suggesting that conservative and socialist positions are the same, but rather that a significant measure of overlap now exists between them. An absolutist definition of culture tied to a resolute defence of the idea of the national community appears uncompromisingly in both.

Themes and concepts which parallel the outpourings of the new racists have appeared in the political pronouncements of many of Britain's black cultural nationalists. Often, the theories and preoccupations of the white racists have simply been inverted to form a thoroughly pastoral account of black culture. This has been combined with an extreme version of cultural relativism which relies for its effect on a volkish ethnic absolutism. Here too the family is seen as the key unit out of which nationality is built, as well as the central means of cultural reproduction.

Where the racists have measured black households against the idealized nuclear family form and found them wanting,[16] this black politics has viewed black children as the primary resource of the 'race' with predictable consequences, particularly in terms of the continued subordination of women. Where this tendency is strongest, particularly in local government agencies where black professionals have been able to consolidate their power, a special concern with black fostering and adoption policy has emerged as the primary vehicle for black cultural nationalism. This issue has precipitated a debate over the capacity of white families to provide an environment in which black culture and identity can be nurtured. It has achieved a symbolic currency far beyond its immediate institutional context. An absolutist conception of cultural or ethnic difference appears here to underpin the fear that new forms of slavery are being created in the placement of black children in white families for adoption or fostering and the consequent belief that racial identity necessarily overrides all other considerations. The class character of the political formation organized around this ideology cannot be elaborated here. However, it would appear that these potent symbols of a racial community and its beleaguered boundaries play an important role in securing the unity of an emergent black *petit bourgeois* and in mystifying their intrinsically problematic relationship to those they are supposed to serve, particularly in a social-work setting. Belief in the transcendental racial essence capable of uniting the black professionals with their dispossessed black clients, conjures away awkward economic and historical complexities and occludes the conspicuous divergence of interests between the never-employed and the cadre of black bureaucrats employed by the local state to salve their misery.

This divergence within the black communities is significant because the logic of Britain's crisis is itself a logic of cultural and political fragmentation. The recent history of race politics can be identified by the decomposition of open, inclusive definitions of 'blackness' which facilitated political alliances by accommodating the discontinuous histories of Afro-Caribbean and Asian descended people, The more restrictive definitions which emerged to take their place and restrict the term 'black' to those of Afro-Caribbean ancestry betoken a general retreat into the dubious comfort of ethnic particularity. However, this fracturing process is far more extensive than its intra-ethnic dimensions suggest. The economic effects of the crisis are, for example, unevenly developed in the most radical manner; they are unevenly distributed even within the same city. It has become commonplace to speak of Britain as two nations – an exploited and immiserated north bearing the brunt of de-industrialization, and a more affluent south. These definitions of the nation are more than competing metaphors. They correspond to important changes in the mode of production itself and the geography of class formation and political representation. The Labour Party presides over the north and the inner cities almost without challenge. The Conservatives enjoy a similar monopoly of power in the more prosperous and suburban areas. Amidst these divisions, to answer the pleas for aid from the ailing north, where notions of region and locality have provided an important axis of political organization, with the language of nationalism and patriotism, is fundamentally misguided. The racial connotations which emerge with this rhetoric work actively to distance black citizens from the system of formal politics as a whole. The counter-position of local and national identities makes nonsense of the idea of a homogenous national culture. The intensity with which it has emerged as a political problem suggests a deeper crisis of the nation-state.

Elsewhere in *Towards 2000* Williams has suggestively described the nation-state as being simultaneously both too large and too small a unit for the necessary forms of political interaction required by the advancement of radical democracy during the years ahead. Seeing the nation as a totality of different societies constructed for different purposes allows us to ask how these may learn to co-exist, and in particular, what role the cultural politics of Britain's black settlers and their British-born children may play in creating a pluralistic ambience in which people are able to discover positive pleasure in their inescapable diversity.

An understanding of the limitations of the nation-state as a form is central to the sense of the African diaspora as a cultural and political unit which anchors black English political culture. The majority of Britain's blacks are post-war settlers but their refined diaspora awareness is more than a reflection of the proximity of migration. It corresponds directly to the subordinate position which Britain's small and diverse black population has occupied within the vast network of cultural and political exchange which links blacks in Africa, the Caribbean, the United States and Europe. Until very recently, this country's identifiably black culture has been created from the raw materials supplied by blacks elsewhere, particularly in America and the Caribbean.

In one sense, the political network which made this cultural relationship possible was a direct product of the commercial traffic in slaves. The activities of eighteenth- and nineteenth-century abolitionists, the transnational and international organization of anti-slavery activities and pan-African initiatives[17] prepared the way for the great gains of the Garvey movement. Each of these phases of black self-organization consolidated independent means of communication between the different locations within the diaspora. What principally concerns us here is the cultural character of these developments: the special premium they have placed on expressive culture – music, song and dance. Artistic forms have produced and sustained an interpretive community outside the orbit of formal politics in a long sequence of struggles which has been irreducibly and simultaneously both cultural and political. The internationalization of the leisure industries and the growth of important markets for cultural commodities outside the overdeveloped world has provided new opportunities for the consolidation of diaspora awareness. The popular pan-Africanist and Ethiopianist visions inherent in reggae were, for example, carried to all the corners of the world as an unforeseen consequence of selling the music of

Jamaica beyond the area in which it was created. The ideologies and sign systems of Afro-American Black Power in part travelled by a similar route. The narrow nationalism we saw in the politics of the emergent black *petit bourgeois* contrasts sharply with the voice of the social movement which has been articulated through the language, styles and symbols of the diaspora. Britain's black population is comparatively small and heterogeneous. Britain has no ghettos along the American model or any residential communities comparable to Bantustans and squatter camps of South Africa. The blackest areas of the inner city are, for example, between 30 and 50 per cent white. Here, the idea of the black community necessarily expresses something more than just the physical concentration of black people. The term has a special moral valency and refers above all to a community of interpretation whose cultural cohesion has sometimes enabled it to act politically. This is a community bounded by language and by cultural forms which play an ethical and educative role. Although the collapse of certainties once provided by class identity, class politics and class theory has been a pronounced feature of the recent period in Britain, it is also a community which has been articulated at a number of points, with the contemporary structures of class relations. In the encounter between black settlers and their white inner-city neighbours, black culture has become a class culture. There is more to this transformation and adaptation than the fact that blacks are among the most economically exploited and politically marginal sections of the society, over-represented in the surplus population, the prison population and among the poor. From the dawn of post-war settlement, diaspora culture has been an ambiguous presence in the autonomous institutions of the working class. Two generations of whites have appropriated it, discovering in its seductive forms meanings of their own. It is now impossible to speak coherently of black culture in Britain in isolation from the culture of Britain as a whole. This is particularly true as far as leisure is concerned. Black expressive culture has decisively shaped youth culture, pop culture and the culture of city life in Britain's metropolitan centres. The white working class has danced for forty years to its syncopated rhythms. There is, of course, no contradiction between making use of black culture and loathing real live black people, yet the informal, long-term processes through which different groups have negotiated each other have intermittently created a 'two-tone' sensibility which celebrates its hybrid origins and has provided a significant opposition to 'common-sense' racialism.

It is often argued that the spontaneity of black musical forms, their performance aesthetic and commitment to improvisation have made them into something of a magnet for other social groups. Certainly the centrality that issues of sexuality, eroticism and gender conflict enjoy within black folk cultures has given them a wide constituency. Their Rabelaisian power to carnivalize and disperse the dominant order through an intimate yet public discourse on sexuality and the body has drawn many outsiders into a dense complex network of black cultural symbols. These aspects of black forms mark out a distinct field of political antagonisms which I do not intend to examine here. Instead, I want to explore the equally distinctive *public* political character of these forms and the urban social movement they have helped to create and extend.

The politics of this movement are manifested in the confluence of three critical, anti-capitalist themes which have an historic resonance in diaspora culture and can be traced directly and indirectly back to the formative experience of slavery. Together they form a whole but non-programmatic politics which has sustained Britain's black settler populations and their white inner-city associates. The first theme deals with the experience of work, the labour process and the division of labour under capitalism. It amounts to a critique of productivism – the ideology which sees the expansion of productive forces as an indispensable precondition of the attainment of freedom. In opposition to this view of production, an argument is made which sees waged work as itself a form of servitude. At best, it is viewed as a necessary evil and is sharply counterposed to the more authentic freedoms which can only be enjoyed in non-work time. The black body is here celebrated as an instrument of pleasure rather than an instrument of labour. The night time becomes the right time and the space allocated for recovery and recuperation is assertively and provocatively occupied by the pursuit of leisure and pleasure.

The second theme focuses on the state. It addresses the role of law in particular and, in challenging capitalist legality to live up to the expansive promises of its democratic rhetoric, articulates a plea for the dissociation of law from the processes of domination. The legal institutions on which Babylon's order of public authority rest do not provide equal rights for all. The version of justice they peddle is partial and inseparable from the system of economic interests which capitalist legality simply guarantees. The coercive brutality of the state is seen as an intrinsic property of these institutions. The exterminism and militarism that characterizes them are denounced, not only where they reach into people's lives as the police or army but for the way that they symbolize the illegitimate nature of the capitalist state in general. This mystified form of rule is unfavourably compared to two quite different standards of justice: first, a divine version which will ultimately redress the miscarriages of earthly 'man-made' law, and second, an alternative secular moral standard – truth and right – which derives its legitimate power from popular sovereignty. It is significant that capitalist legality is understood to have denied blacks the status of legal subjects during the slave period.

The third theme concentrates on the importance of history understood as a discontinuous process of struggle. An affirmation of history and the place of blacks within it is advanced as an antidote to the suppression of temporal perception under capitalism. This theme also answers the way in which racism works to suppress the historical dimensions of black life, offering a mode of existence locked permanently into a recurrent present where social existence is confined to the roles of being either a problem or a victim.

The contemporary musical forms of the African diaspora work within an aesthetic and political framework which demands that they ceaselessly reconstruct their own histories, folding back on themselves time and again to celebrate and validate the simple, unassailable fact of their survival. This is particularly evident in jazz, where quotes from and parody of earlier styles and performers make the past actually audible in the present. This process of recovery should not be misunderstood. It does not amount to either parody or pastiche. The stylistic voices of the past are valued for the distinct register of address which each offers. The same playful process is evident in the less abstract performances which define Washington's 'Go Go' dance funk. This style consists of a continuous segue from one tune to the next. The popular black musics of different eras and continents are wedded together by a heavy percussive rhythm and an apparently instinctive antiphony. A recent concert in London by Chuck Brown, the kingpin of the Go Go, saw him stitch together tunes by Louis Jordan, Sly Stone, Lionel Hampton, Melle Mel and T Bone Walker into a single epic statement. Reggae's endless repetition of 'versions' and the tradition of answer records in rhythm and blues betray a similar historical impulse.

The core themes I have identified overlap and interact to generate a cohesive but essentially defensive politics and a corresponding aesthetic of redemption from racial subordination.

The critique of productivism is reinforced and extended by the structural location of black labour power in Britain and the other overdeveloped countries. It is also tied to the movement among young blacks which actively rejects the menial and highly exploitative forms in which work is made available. The concern with history demands that the experience of slavery is also recovered and rendered vivid and immediate. It becomes a powerful metaphor for the injustice and exploitation of contemporary waged work in general.

The anti-capitalist politics which animate the social movement against racial subordination is not confined to the lyrical content of these musical cultures. The poetics involved recurrently deals with these themes but the critique of capitalism is simultaneously revealed in the forms which this expressive culture takes and in the performance aesthetic which governs them. There is here an imminent challenge to the commodity form to which black expressive culture is reduced in order to be sold. It is a challenge that is practised rather than simply talked or sung about. The artefacts of a pop industry premised on the individual act of purchase and consumption are hijacked and taken over into the heart of collective rituals of protest and affirmation which in turn define the boundaries of the interpretive community. Music is heard socially and its deepest meanings revealed only in the heat of this collective, affirmative consumption. Struggles over the commodification of black music are reflected in a dialectical conflict between the technology of reproduction and the sub-cultural needs of its primary consumers in the 'race market'. Here, the pioneering use of live recordings occupying the whole side of a long-playing disc, issuing the same song in two parts on different sides of a 45 and putting out various different mixes of a song on one 12-inch disc to facilitate scratch mixing are all part of the story. Musicians and producers for whom the 'race market' is the primary constituency are reluctant to compromise with the commercial formats that the music business relies on. Where they are able to exercise control over the form in which their music is issued, black artists anticipate this specific mode of consumption and privilege it. Records are issued in an open, participative form which invites further artistic input. The Toaster or MC adds rhymes and comments to the wordless version of a tune which is routinely issued on the reverse of the vocal version. Several different versions of the same piece are issued on a single record; 12-inch discs which allow for extended playing time are favoured. Thus the original artefact negotiates the supplementary input of other artists unseen and unknown yet anticipated by the original creator of the music.

The clubs, parties and dances where these creative negotiations between original and supplementary performances take place are governed by a dramaturgy which prizes the local, immediate and seemingly spontaneous input above all. Leaving behind the passive role of spectator to which they would be assigned by Western convention, these audiences instead become active participants. In this metaphysics of intimacy, 'race' mediates the social relation between internal pain and its externalization in cathartic performance. The audience's association with the performer dissolves Eurocentric notions of the disjunction between art and life, inside and outside, in the interplay of personal and public histories for which the traditions of the black church serve as a model and an inspiration.[18]

The complex, dialogic rituals involved become sources of profound pleasure in their own right, particularly where singers and musicians encounter a crowd directly. The musical counter-cultures of black Britain are primarily based around records rather than live performances but the same aesthetic of performance applies. Music recorded on discs loses its pre-ordained authority as it is transformed and adapted. In reggae, soul and hip-hop

sub-cultures the disc which appears in the dominant culture as a
fixed and final product is extended and reconstructed as it
becomes the raw material in a new creative process born in the
dialogue between the DJ, the rapper or MC and the dancing
crowd. A range of de/reconstructive procedures – scratch mixing, dubbing, toasting, rapping and beatboxing – contribute to
new layers of local meaning. The original performance trapped
in plastic is supplemented by new contributions at every stage.
Performer and audience alike strive to create pleasures that can
evade capture and sale as cultural commodities. A hostility to
commercial trafficking in black music has grown so steadily that
the majority of black clubs and leisure spaces are actively disin-
terested in the latest new records, forsaking them in favour of
old and hard-to-obtain discs in an anti-aesthetic cult known as
the 'rare groove' scene. Popularized by the illegal pirate radio
stations which deal exclusively in the various styles of black
music, this fashion has placed a special premium on politically
articulate American dance-funk recordings from the Black
Power period. Because it cannot be bought, the pleasures in
hearing a particular tune are severed from the commercial relations of pop. Dislocated from the time and place in which they
were created, discs like Hank Ballard's 1968 'How You Gonna
Get Respect? You Haven't Cut Your Process Yet'[19] become
abstract metaphysical statements on the nature of blackness.
The same process applies to music imported into Britain's black
communities from the Caribbean. Again for both reggae- and
soul-based traditions, the polysemic qualities of black speech
add to the subversive potency of the DJ's and MC's language
games.

These issues can be examined further by considering the
impact of 'I Know You Got Soul', an American hip-hop record
which was the most popular item in London's black clubs for
several months at the beginning of 1987. The record was a new

version of Bobby Byrd's sixteen-year-old Black Power anthem. Snatches of his original version were still clearly audible but it had been transformed by the addition of a drum machine and an unusually clever and poetic rap. Eric B and Rakim, the creators of the new version, declared themselves emphatically committed to a ghetto constituency, people who, as Rakim put it when I spoke to him, 'turn to music because they got nothin' else'. The record affirms this commitment by celebrating the concept of soul which is thought to be fundamental to black experience, 'You listen to it . . . the concept might break you.' Its dense, dizzy sound privileges and anticipates a public hearing: 'Sit by the radio hand on the dial, soon as you hear it pump up the volume.' But the public sphere to which it is addressed is defined against the dominant alternative to which blacks enjoy only restricted access. This is an altogether different forum, bounded by the strictures of race and community and marked out by the naming process which gave these young men their identity as performers. The soul power that the record manifests is also the force that binds their listeners together into a moral, even a political community. For black Britain constructing its own distinct culture from material supplied by the United States and the Caribbean, 'I Know You Got Soul' brilliantly tied a sense of exclusive contemporary style to an older, positive message of self-respect and political autonomy which derives its power from the American black movement of the 1960s. The disc, an adaptation and transformation of an earlier piece that retained the original within its own fractured form, was scratched, dubbed and made over time and time again in the dancehalls, parties and other leisure spaces of Britain's black community. Its consumption by Afro-Caribbean and Asian descended Britons and their white friends, lovers and associates defined the boundaries of a utopian social movement. This movement aims to defend and extend spaces for social autonomy and meets the oppressive power of racial capitalism with the radical aspiration that one day work will no longer be servitude and law no longer equated with domination. Thus the territoriality of identity is counter-posed to the territoriality of control. An immediate, non-negotiable politics is infused with a powerful sense of locality and a rootedness in tradition, 'It ain't where you're from,' intones Rakim, 'it's where you're at.'

It is interesting to note that, at the very moment when celebrated Euro-American cultural theorists have pronouced the collapse of 'grand narratives', the expressive culture of Britain's black poor is dominated by the need to construct them as narratives of redemption and emancipation. This expressive culture, like others elsewhere in the African diaspora, produces a potent historical memory and an authoritative analytical and historical account of racial capitalism and its overcoming. There are of course many problems in trying to hold the term 'post-modernism' together. It refers simultaneously and contradictorily to modernization, to a cognitive theory, to a change in the cultural climate in the overdeveloped countries and to an aspect of the logic of late capitalism. The concept may have some value as a purely heuristic device but it often seems simply to serve to validate another equally Eurocentric master narrative from which the history and experiences of blacks remain emphatically absent. Fredric Jameson,[20] for example, views post-modernism as 'the cultural dominant'. However, all the constitutive features of the post-modern that he identifies – the new depthlessness, the weakening of historicity, the waning of affect – are not merely absent from black expressive cultures but are explicitly contradicted by their repertoire of complete 'hermeneutic gestures'. These cultural forms use the new technological means at their disposal not to flee from depth but to revel in it, not to abjure public history but to proclaim it! This cultural politics is not about the waning of affect but about its reproduction, and its creators have forged their own thoroughly subversive means to inhabit what Jameson calls 'the bewildering new world space of late multi-national capital'.

There is, in the history of these forms, a suggestion that the grand narrative of reason is not being brought to an end but itself transformed, democratized and extended. This transformation, which sees the centre of ethical gravity shift away from 'the West', is mistakenly identified as the end of reason. Forms of rationality are being created endlessly. The post-modernists' claim that the present moment is *the* moment of rupture contains echoes of earlier European obsessions with the precise timing of the new dawn. Rather than seek to substitute an aesthetic radicalism for a moral one, as many spokespeople for post-modernism have implicitly and explicitly suggested, the expressive culture shows how these two dimensions can be aligned in a complex sensibility sometimes utopian, sometimes fiercely pragmatic.

The movement it articulates has coalesced somewhere between what Jean Cohen has called the 'identity-oriented' and 'resource-mobilization' paradigms for comprehending social action.[21] It is neither a class nor, of course, a racially homogenous grouping. Its identity is a product of immediate local circumstances but is apprehended through a syncretic culture for which the history of the African diaspora supplies the decisive symbolic core. Partly because religious language conveys an intensity of aspiration for which there is no secular alternative, this culture has a spiritual component. As we have already seen, it views the body as itself an important locus of resistance and desire. The body is therefore reclaimed from its subordination to the labour process, recognized as part of the natural world and enjoyed on that basis. Third, and most importantly, this movement can be identified by its antipathy to the institutions of formal politics and the fact that it is not principally oriented towards instrumental objectives. Rather than aim at the conquest of political power or apparatuses, its objective centres on the control of a field of autonomy or independence from the system.

The distinctive political perspective that emerges from this movement can lead us to a more scrupulous and detailed periodization of modernity itself. The modernizing processes in which commodification and industrialization come together with the political institutions of formal democracy have had *regional* as well as temporal characteristics. It is therefore useful to reconceptualize the struggles of African diaspora populations not simply as anti-capitalist but as a product of one of modernity's most significant and enduring counter-cultures. Capitalism, industrialization and their political counterparts are differentiated and then analysed in their articulation. The social movement which is the contemporary heir to a non-European radical tradition[22] has a more total critique of them than that currently spoken in furtherance of the struggle to emancipate labour from capital.

Identifying this radical tradition, unburdened by the dream of progress and a positivistic faith in the easy certainties of Marxian science, returns us to the question of whose master narratives are collapsing and whose growing stronger? This inquiry in turn provides a further cue to shift the centre of debate away from Europe, and to explore other encounters with modernity which a dogmatic post-modern perspective ignores or dismisses as peripheral. As C. L. R. James[23] argued long ago, the history of communism ought to reckon with political communities for whom the 'enthusiasm of 1789' relates to Port au Prince before it relates to Paris. Why is it so difficult to think through the relationship between them? These problems have been the substance of diaspora culture through slavery and since. The people whom June Jordan has eloquently called 'the stubborn majority of this world'[24] have had a variety of complex and problematic relationships to 'modernity'. This has been true from the moment when Africans, detached from an identifiable location in space and time, became negroes – in the West but not organically of it – and acquired the 'double vision' which a subordinate position entails. As slaves, their exclusion from universal human categories demanded the acquisition and validation of an authentic humanity. It is also relevant that their experiences as unfree working populations engaged in industrial capitalist production have been accorded secondary status behind those of the industrial proletariat by four generations of Marxist theoreticians.

Questions of political economy aside, studying the distinct 'intertextual' traditions of the African diaspora alone demands extensive adjustments to the conceptualization of modernization, modernity and aesthetic modernism. The idea of a 'populist' modernism is a useful preliminary means to comprehend the cultural and political strategies which have evolved not only where European philosophy and letters have been bent to other purposes by Nella Larsen, Richard Wright, James Baldwin, David Bradley, Alice Walker or most self-consciously in Amiri Baraka's black Baudelaire, but to make sense of the secular and spiritual *popular* forms – music and dance which have handled the anxieties and dilemmas involved in a response to the flux of modern life.

The cultural politics of 'race' can be more accurately described as the cultural politics of racism's overcoming. It challenges theories which assert the primacy of structural contradictions, economic classes and crises in determining political consciousness and collective action. Traditions of radical politics arising from groups whose enduring jeopardy dictates that the premises of their social existence are threatened, may in our post-industrial era be more radical than more obviously class-based modes of political action. The high level of support for the striking miners and their families inside Britain's black communities during the recent coal dispute seems to indicate that these different varieties of radicalism can be brought together. During that industrial dispute, highly dissimilar groups were able to connect their fates across the divisions of 'race', ethnicity, region and language. For a brief period, inner-city populations and the vanguard of the orthodox industrial proletariat shrank the world to the size of their immediate communities and began, in concert, to act politically on that basis. In doing so, they supplied a preliminary but nonetheless concrete answer to the decisive political questions of our age: how do we act locally and yet think globally? How do we connect the local and the immediate across the earthworks erected by the division of labour?

Notes

I would like to thank Vron Ware and Mandy Rose for their help with this essay.

1. Some of the themes and problems discussed in this piece have been elaborated in my book *There Ain't No Black in the Union Jack: The Cultural Politics of Race and Nation*, Hutchinson, London, 1987.
2. One version of this problematic appears in the work of Stuart Hall, particularly his 1980 paper 'Race, Articulation and Societies Structured in Dominance', published in the Unesco reader *Sociological Theories: Race and Colonialism*, Paris. See also his 'Signification, Representation, Ideology: Althusser and the post-structuralist debates' in *Critical Studies in Mass Communication*, vol. 2, no. 2, June 1985. A similar position is sketched on somewhat different ground by Alex Callinicos in his 'Postmodernism, Post-Structuralism and Post-Marxism?', *Theory, Culture and Society*, vol. 2, no. 2, 1985. Both pieces draw heavily on the work of Volosinov/Bakhtin.
3. 'The Voiceless Ones', *Saturday Review*, 16 April 1960.
4. I am thinking here of Robert Miles's *Racism and Migrant Labour*, RKP,

London, 1982, and John Gabriel and Gideon Ben Tovim's essay 'Marxism and the Concept of Racism', *Economy and Society*, vol. 7, no. 2, May 1978.

5. Hall, 'Racism and Moral Panics in Post-war Britain' in Commission for Racial Equality (ed.), *Five Views of Multi-racial Britain*, London, 1978.

6. *Shamanism, Colonialism and the Wild Men: A Study in Terror and Healing*, University of Chicago Press, 1987. Michael Taussig's absolutely brilliant study of race and colonial terror is an excellent example of what can be achieved. Less inspiring but worth investigating nonetheless are Orlando Patterson's *Ethnic Chauvinism: The Reactionary Impulse*, Stein and Day, New York, 1977, and Anthony D. Smith's *The Ethnic Revival in the Modern World*, Cambridge University Press, 1981.

7. Andrew Gamble, *Britain in Decline*, Macmillan, London, 1981.

8. Apart from *There Ain't No Black*, see CCCS (eds), *The Empire Strikes Back*, Hutchinson, London, 1982, and S. Hall et al., *Policing the Crisis*, Macmillan, London, 1979.

9. Nancy Stepan, *The Idea of Race in Science: Great Britain 1800–1960*, Macmillan, London, 1982.

10. Frantz Fanon, *Toward the African Revolution*, Pelican, Harmondsworth, 1967.

11. A useful account of the development of the English New Right is provided in R. Levitas (ed.), *The Ideology of the New Right*, Polity, Oxford, 1985. See also *The New Right Enlightenment: Young Writers on the Spectre Haunting the Left*, Economic and Literary Books, Sevenoaks, 1985. The men referred to here are part of an influential grouping around the journal *Salisbury Review*. Ray Honeyford in particular became something of a celebrity when he opposed the introduction of 'anti-racist and multi-cultural' teaching methods into the inner-city school where he was headmaster.

12. See Vron Ware, *Beyond the Pale: White Women, Racism and History*, Verso, London, 1992.

13. Frank Palmer (ed.), *Anti-racism: An Assault on Education and Value*, Sherwood Press, London, 1986.

14. See Patrick Wright's *On Living in an Old Country*, Verso, London, 1985.

15. Raymond Williams, *Towards 2000*, Chatto, London, 1983.

16. A concern with the supposedly pathological forms in which black family life develops is shared by Lord Scarman's report into the 1981 riots in London and Daniel Moynihan's report *The Negro Family and the Case for National Action*. This convergence and the image of family breakdown in racist ideology is discussed by Errol Lawrence in the CCCS volume *The Empire Strikes Back*.

17. I am thinking here of the settlement of Sierra Leone and of the travels of black abolitionists in Britain and Europe. On the latter, see C. Peter Ripley (ed.), *The Black Abolitionist Papers*, vol. 1, University of North Carolina Press, 1985, and Clare Taylor (ed.), *British and American Abolitionists*, Edinburgh University Press, 1974. For Sierra Leone, see Immanuel Geiss,

The Pan-African Movement, Methuen, London, 1974.

18. Gerald L. Davis, *I Got the Word in Me and I Can Sing It, You Know: A Study of the Performed African-American Sermon*, University of Pennsylvania Press, 1985.

19. Hank Ballard and The Dapps, 'How You Gonna Get Respect?', King Records, K6196. The cut is also included on the 1969 album 'You Can't Keep A Good Man Down', King, K1052.

20. Fredric Jameson, 'Postmodernism or the Cultural Logic of Late Capitalism', *New Left Review*, vol. 146, July/August 1984.

21. Jean Cohen, 'Strategy or Identity: New theoretical paradigms and contemporary social movements', *Social Research*, vol. 52, no. 4, Winter 1985.

22. Cedric J. Robinson, *Black Marxism: The Making of the Black Radical Tradition*, Zed Press, London, 1982.

23. C. L. R. James, *The Black Jacobins*, Allison and Busby, London, 1980.

24. June Jordan, *Civil Wars*, Beacon Press, Boston, 1981.

2 The peculiarities of the black English

All nations are, in Benedict Anderson's words, 'imaginary communities'. Their existence and continuity cannot simply be assumed. They are not spontaneously formed and although they sometimes appear to us as if they are natural or eternal associations, they have been constructed through elaborate cultural, ideological and political processes which culminate in the feeling of connectedness to other national subjects and in the idea of a national interest that transcends the supposedly petty divisions of class, region, dialect or caste.

In recent years, the structure of European nation-states has come under great strain. Nation states may be waning in their significance but nationalism is certainly not dying with them. It is being reborn in all manner of unexpected and barbarous configurations. The idea of nationality has, for example, acquired a new appeal to some peoples who have had limited experience of the nation-state as a democratic political structure. They want their own national units but they want them to be pure and culturally homogenous.

This chapter was a paper for the conference on Race, Cultural Production and Everyday Life, organized by Flemming Røgilds and held at the University of Copenhagen in May 1989. A slightly different version was published in *Every Cloud Has a Silver Lining*, the volume of conference proceedings.

Britain has experienced similar tensions at a special, post-imperial intensity produced under the impact of both internal and external forces. The internal ones stem from the conflicts that have grown out of hostile responses to mass economic immigration during the post-war years. This was a pattern of immigration in which citizenship rights were widely and freely granted but then steadily chipped away until 1971, when primary settlement ended. The external ones derive from the British nation's transformed position in the world and the economic, political and cultural adjustments which have had to be made in order to accept the simple and brute fact that this country is no longer a major world power. These pressures have been shaped by a process of fragmentation that has an economic aspect but which is much more than narrowly economic. It is a whole, cultural experience in which system crisis and lived crisis are closely articulated.

Externally, the ambiguous lure of a wider European identity and the power of transnational and multinational structures like NATO and the EC have bitten deep into the time-worn 'wogs begin at Calais' mentality of the old 'Little Englanders'. Capital has begun to organize its activities in new patterns that take them far beyond the grasp of national governments and although this has different effects in different sectors of production, it marks a decisive change. Labour, hampered by its own historic distaste for the effeminate French, the cowardly Italians and the militaristic Germans, has slowly and grudgingly begun to produce a new strategy which identifies the party as more European than the governments it has opposed.

Since 1979, the Conservative governments have pursued a new policy of linkages with world capital which has had a significant impact on conceptions of national sovereignty. Their early ending of exchange controls in 1979 pointed to an intense desire to make London into a world financial centre – overseas firms, governments and individuals now account for some 75 per cent of all financial deposits in the United Kingdom. Internally, the polity have had to make sense of a slow but relentless economic decline which has destroyed our manufacturing base in favour of an expanded financial sector. The impact of these changes has been effectively concealed by the revenues from North Sea oil. It will be impossible to overlook now that the oil has run out.

This paper is primarily concerned with some of the political and ideological counterparts to the processes of economic transformation that I have only hinted at. These have seen dissensus emerge from the rubble of a post-war bipartisanship in which race and immigration were central themes. Britain has also had to contend with a government of the extreme right, which has prided itself on an openly *populist* orientation to political life which marks a clean break with older patrician habits inside the Conservative Party. This is where what was called Thatcherism began, and the ideas of 'race' and nation, of England and Englishness, have pride of place within it.

The distinctively populist approach of the British new right has made history and the sense of the national past an important political issue. Anyone visiting our country will be struck immediately by the national obsession which has turned museums and heritage sites into a boom industry. Political debates are regularly displaced into bitter controversies over the politics of preservationism or the public value of neo-Georgian architecture. The spoof classicism of Quinlan Terry has ironically become a potent symbol of the virtues of tradition and an emblem for authentic national culture. The well-publicized interventions of Prince Charles in this area are only the most superficial examples of a volatile situation in which symbols of a pre-modern, even explicitly feudal, past are frequently invoked to hold the flux of the post-modern present at bay. The wholesale restructuring of Britain's welfare state, for example, is perversely presented to the electorate in the guise of a liberatory *modernization* of institutions that have long outlived their usefulness. At the same time, the long-suffering Labour Party has been identified as the instigator of inhuman modernist housing projects in the inner city while the Conservative Government, in their familiar anti-urban regalia, are seen as the party of the civilized rural alternative – the stately home.

One effect of the populist turn has been a highly charged *politics of identity* which has appeared both at the very core of the official political culture and, of course, in popular culture too. The war in the South Atlantic in the early 1980s was only the most obvious sign of the extent to which Britons had suddenly became rather unsure of who they were! War is, of course, a crucial process in clarifying the issue of national membership. It defines in an instant the scope and status of the national community. Britain's victories in the two world wars are cherished alongside our triumph in the 1966 World Cup by young men who intersperse their 'traditional' litany of sexual and racial abuse with alternate appeals to the spirits of Hitler and Churchill.

This year (1990) marks fifty years since the Battle of Britain and the memory of World War II is already being reawakened to serve some dismal political purposes. We are being invited to don our tin hats and descend once again into the air-raid shelters where the national character was tempered by adversity. The imagery of the nation at war is everywhere and it derives a great deal of its power from representing Britain as a homogeneous community undivided by race or culture – prior to the steady decline initiated by black settlement in the immediate aftermath of the conflict. Apart from recovering the war itself in increasingly vulgar and desperate forms, the analogy of war is growing more and more common in political discourses of all kinds. It is now applied routinely to the national moral panics which emerge with extraordinary regularity – labour disputes, child

abuse in the family, drugs, even the role of the Church in political life, and, above all, in and around the issue of race. In all
these areas of conflict the idea of the nation and the cohesiveness
of national identity are shown to be under attack from dark,
subversive and sinister forces – an Enemy Within.

It is worth emphasizing that these assaults on the national
community are perceived to be simultaneously both political and
cultural. They take a variety of forms not all of which are
directly related to the experience and history of Britain's black
settlers. For example, reflecting the unevenness of economic crisis in productive institutions, we have come routinely to speak of
two nations – the affluent, silicon South and the once-industrial
North where the impact of structural unemployment has been
greatest. Demands for political autonomy from the United
Kingdom's various national groups are also important here – the
low-intensity war in Ireland, Welsh nationalism, Scots nationalism and the absence of the Tory mandate north of the border all
point to the possibility that Britain is not in fact a unified nation
at all but rather a *state* which links together a number of ethnic
and linguistic groups whose histories are as discontinuous as
their needs are discrepant. This process of cultural and political
fragmentation forms the context in which I now want to try to
locate the related but rather separate conflicts around 'race' and
the black presence.

In raising the issue of race, it is essential that you understand
that I am not speaking of a newly immigrant population. Nor do
I mean to refer you exclusively to the defensive cultural and
political struggles of the black settlers and their British-born children. I believe that these cannot be considered in isolation from
the racial consciousness and outlook of the majority population,
many of whom comfort themselves from the chill winds of the
crisis with an anachronistic but nonetheless potent belief in the
imperial missions of the past and the belief in a 'white' race

which derives from it. In very different ways for both blacks *and* whites, the idea of race becomes a fundamental aspect of their response to the turbulence of economic and cultural crisis – providing a chain of meaning which makes the process of national decline intelligible as a whole. We shall see in a moment that this can happen even where the term 'race' is not itself used. England is, of course, somewhere which has a special place within the African diaspora, standing at the apex of the old triangular network of trade and the unforeseen political relationships which that has produced.

The black experience in England is increasingly revealed to possess a certain uniqueness – a particularity and peculiarity that distinguish it from the history of black populations elsewhere in the diaspora. The concept of diaspora has become a useful one because it allows us to look simultaneously at the differences and the continuities in black experience. You may know that this country has had a black population for over 400 years but the bulk of the contemporary black population is the product of post-war settlement. This means that many of our racial problems stem from the brevity rather than the longevity of our stay in the overdeveloped world. There was no plantation slavery in Britain itself and it is therefore the experience of migration and our post-colonial position rather than the memory of slavery which form the basic unifying experiences for us. The oldest black populations are found around the great ports of the eighteenth century – Liverpool, Cardiff, Bristol and London – but these older groups are different from post-war economic migrants. They may not, for example, have lines of descent from the Caribbean and intimate relationships with whites may be more common. The size and heterogeneity of Britain's black populations are also relevant here. There are significant differences of language, religion, ethnicity and culture evident within this population. In recent years it has come to be increasingly internally divided. It is economically stratified and politically split. Most important for political purposes is the experiential and cultural divergence between 'Afro-Caribbean' populations and 'Asian' ones. Some of the latter were indentured in the Caribbean after abolition, some came directly from various parts of the Indian sub-continent while others came to the mother country from Kenya and Uganda. They too are divided by language, religion and ethnicity to a point where the label 'Asian' itself is fundamentally misleading. This problem of political language is again expressed in the way that the term 'black' has been employed intermittently to take in the experience of these different groups. This has emerged as a controversial issue. For some, the emptiness of the term in contrast to the alternative 'African' creates problems, while from within 'Asian' communities there has been a degree of resistance to the idea that the concept can be used politically rather than descriptively.

The unique forms of racism that structure our lives also have an impact on the cohesiveness and political identity of Britain's blacks. Racism may constitute a kind of centripetal force but it is as likely to separate as it is to unify. It affects the different groups in different ways. There is a theoretical lesson here, namely the need to speak of racism(s) in the plural rather than of one racism singular, unchanging and final. This means that the differences between various racisms have to be very clearly specified, for they are not only different between societies but also within them. Earlier imperial forms may, for example, contradict or qualify more recent variations premised on the loss of empire. The racism of the imperial heyday was formed when half the map of the world was still painted pink. It cannot be the same as racism bred in conditions of decline and economic instability. Indeed the contemporary variety of racism is so different from its precursors that some of us began, loosely and heuristically, to call it the *new racism*.

The old racism stressed the ideology of an imperial family of nations. This has been replaced by an ideology of Britain as a nation of families. The old racism said 'keep them out'; the new says 'send them back' instead. The old took an economic, *laissez-faire* approach to the issue of black citizenship, whereas the new is premised on the qualification and withdrawal of those rights and entitlements. The old embraced little Englandism, while the new manages to coexist, albeit uneasily, with a wider sense of pan-European identity. An idea of blacks as a problem for the national community supplies the continuity between these two different folk theories of race but the definition of that problem varies. Underlining the movement away from biology and towards culture which also marks the shift from old to new racisms, we British blacks are now a problem, not because of any biological inferiority but because of the extent of the cultural differences which divide us from bona fide Brits. There is no biological hierarchy of races to be found here. Indeed the cultural flavour of today's racism may mean that no mention is made of old-style biological races at all. There are, of course, colour-coded ways of talking about race without using the actual word: the code of the inner city is the most obvious example. But the new racists are able to say quite convincingly that they do not believe in a biological hierarchy of 'racial' groups and that they reject the value of phenotypical variations as a means to classify humanity. This has created a number of profound political and strategic problems for anti-racism. It is also essential to observe here that, from the standpoint of the racially oppressed groups, it does not matter all that much what theory is used to justify the practice of racial terror. Here at least, the agenda of the academy does not coincide tidily with the political agenda set in the streets.

This in turn points to the fact that the new racism accomplishes new political work. I've already mentioned the growth of a self-consciously populist conservatism. Race and the related discourses of nationalism, patriotism and culture have provided important links between that populist impulse and its authoritarian counterpart. What is interesting here is that the concept of culture has become a crucial ground for political struggle. And, as culture has grown more central to political debates on race, it has also become more *reductively* conceived, as if it becomes a biological term through its proximity to the concept of race. In its pre-modern usage, the term 'race' was often a synonym for the contemporary idea of culture. It is not completely surprising, then, that race is now being defined almost exclusively through the ideas of culture and identity. This definition has gained the status of a common-sense explanation for both left and right. In a very worrying development, it has become enshrined as a kind of orthodoxy within organized anti-racism where the simple sum of prejudice and power serves to explain what racism itself is. It is also significant that this new emphasis on culture, nationality and patriotism has taken the new racism beyond the grasp of the old distinction between left and right. Here we should bear in mind that, apart from the problem of working-class racism, Labour has its own nationalist tradition in which both anti-Americanism and hostility to Europe continue to play powerful roles.

The recent controversy over Salman Rushdie's *The Satanic Verses* throws all these issues into stark relief. Many thinkers (of the left) have found their common-sense commitment to a principled form of cultural relativism tested to the limit by the sight of book burnings. These decidedly un-British practices are cited to demonstrate the inappropriate longevity of alien cultures that refuse to fade as well as the folly of the integrationist project. It is particularly interesting that an absolutist sense of ethnic difference regularly goes hand in hand with a cultural relativism of the strongest type.

My fundamental point is that the net effect of the differences between the old and the new varieties of racism can be felt in the way that today's racist ideologies render blackness and Britishness mutually exclusive social and cultural categories. For a long while, the principal way in which all this was played out politically was through the law-and-order issue. The development of more authoritarian governmental styles and institutions politicizes the law in new and unforeseen ways. In these circumstances, law-breaking became identified as an essential and expressive part of the cultural property of black life, a causal element in the same disabling narrative as family pathology, teenage pregnancy, identity crises and intergenerational conflict.

Law-breaking was believed to take culturally specific forms: in particular, street crime. Robbery and rioting were the crimes associated with 'Afro-Caribbeans', while illegal immigration and culturally sanctioned forms of gang activity played the same role for 'Asians'. The importation and abuse of drugs spanned both communities. I am not, of course, saying that these things do not happen but rather querying the way in which they become cultural markers that distinguish one 'racial' group from another and may even specify the distinctive attributes of these groups in public political discourse. These labels and criminal types have a history and I have shown in 'There Ain't No Black in the Union Jack' that for a long time blacks were viewed as a low-crime population. Here too, it is important to appreciate that the aspiring populists of the left share many of the same presuppositions and strategies as the populist right.

Though still in evidence, the law-and-order theme has recently given way to education as the main theme in the populist politics of race. Youth is the link between them. The version of this argument that was centred on law said that crime showed that blacks cannot learn the standards required of authentic English civilization because their cultural equipment is all wrong. The newer permutation of this argument, centred on education, says that blacks do not want to learn the ways of the real English. It suggests that blacks are unaccountably attached to their own religions, languages and norms. And, worse still, they are going to enlist the help of their totalitarian friends in socialist local government agencies to get their proposals turned into policies that can only operate at the expense of the white working class. The school provides a ready image for the nation in microcosm. It is an institution for cultural transmission and therefore a means of integration and assimilation. It hosts two important and related confrontations which have been of great interest to the popular press. The first arises where conflicting cultures have to contend for the attention of the child who may be caught between them, and the second takes shape where the multicultural zealotry of the local authorities who set overall educational policy has had to struggle against the ideologies and politics of heroic, individual teachers who have sought to resist this unwholesome tide of politically motivated zealotry. Mother-tongue teaching, anti-racist and multicultural curricula are all under attack. Twenty years after the modern period in English race relations was inaugurated by a speech prophesying race war, the image of the lone white child in a class full of blacks which was so central to that nightmare vision still makes this theme a public political issue with great popular resonance. You have probably heard of the parents in Dewsbury who withdrew their children from a school where Asians were a majority and sent them to be educated in a pub, and of the tragedy in Burnage where a young Asian boy was murdered in the playground of his school. In the latter case, a moralistic and narrow-minded version of anti-racism was implicated in creating an atmosphere in which the needs of the white children at the school were overlooked.

English cultural studies ought to have had a lot of interesting things to say about the way in which the concept of culture was constructed in these debates. I mentioned earlier that the belief that race could be understood exclusively through the concepts of identity and culture was shared by left and right, black and white. I am not trying to banish culture and identity from discussions about race, but my problem with these arguments is that they close off the possibility that race is an inherently political term. The idea that the groups common-sensically called 'races' are shifting and unstable political collectivities is dismissed or forgotten. Those of you who are concerned to try to think through how race and class might come together will find it significant that the hold of this black cultural nationalism appears to be strongest among the tiny group that might eventually emerge as Britain's black middle class. At present, that group has nothing more than the most preliminary toe-hold in the semi-professions: social work, teaching, local government. The reliance of these posts on the residual structures of the welfare state possibly explains the impulse to draw a veil of spurious ethnic identification over the relationship between black bureaucrats and state functionaries and their racial peers whom they have to serve, police or translate for. However, the reduction of race to culture and identity alone is mistaken for another reason also. Its mystification of the dynamics of racial solidarity and simplification of the complex relationship between race and culture are dangerous. They threaten to turn discussion away from what I regard as the most pressing task, namely producing a political language for dealing with the increasingly important differences that have been apparent within the black communities. We need a better sense of the relationship between these internal differences and the differences that are perceived between racial groups. Do we minimize the former in order to maximize the latter? Holding on tightly to the idea of mutually impermeable ethnic or racial cultures also makes the problem of alliances very difficult. It is unsurprising that in these circumstances the idea of close political unity between 'Asian' and 'Afro-Caribbean' Britons has become more and more unfashionable. It is seen to be illegitimate because it supposedly threatens the integrity of each group.

An alternative view of this issue can be put together through a different view of culture, one which accentuates its plastic, syncretic qualities and which does not see culture flowing into neat ethnic parcels but as a radically unfinished social process of self-definition and transformation. Here, we have to return to the uniqueness of black British cultures. For when racism says that black British culture is a contradiction in terms, even noting that these cultures exist can become a provocative, even subversive, gesture. We must remember too, that black people in this country are a young population and this means that youth culture continues to play a special role in mediating both the racial identities that are freely chosen and the oppressive effects of racism. We must look at the dependent position of black Britain within the African diaspora and at its adaptation and transformation of African-American and Caribbean forms. These cultural borrowings, mixtures and exchanges are frequently reappropriated a second time by the older, urban working-class cultural mainstream and legitimated through the idea of neighbourhood or locality. Our blackest areas are still barely more than 50 per cent non-white. Over the years, these issues have been primarily relevant to the relationship between young whites and 'Afro-Caribbeans' but there are now important signs that similar processes of cultural and linguistic syncretism are beginning to take in 'Asian' culture too. Caribbean and African-American forms are no longer the exclusive raw material for cultural experimentation and synthesis: bhangra has fused traditional Punjabi and Bengali music with hip-hop, soul and house. Extraordinary new forms have been produced and much of their power resides in their capacity to circulate a new sense of what it means to be British. Like their immediate predecessors, American soul and Ethiopianist reggae, these latest hybrid forms will contribute to and take their place within a social movement of urban youth which already has a distinct political ideology. This powerful cultural formation is more than merely defensive and may yet offer a significant alternative to the misery of hard drugs and the radical powerlessness of inner urban life. It was aided by the autonomous illegal broadcasting that has been a notable feature of big-city life in Britain through the 1980s. At their best, these independent cultural institutions represent a utopian extension of the boundaries of politics. They contribute directly to an alternative public sphere, a transfigured public realm to which multinational communicative networks contribute but which they have so far been unable to dominate. These distinctive black British forms have themselves been re-exported to America and the Caribbean. Soul II Soul, who signify much of the maturity and confidence of our vernacular cultural style, have found special favour abroad. The emergent expressive cultures of blacks in Britain have acquired a global profile. The seemingly trivial forms of youth sub-culture point to the opening up of a self-consciously post-colonial space in which the affirmation of difference points forward to a more pluralistic conception of nationality and perhaps beyond that to its transcendence.

3 Nationalism, history and ethnic absolutism

I have been set up here in a sense as an opponent of national history. I wish to decline that role. I am not happy about focusing our discussion through a narrow, for-or-against debate over the writing of something called national history. I would prefer that we move instead to a consideration of *nationalism* as it has a bearing on the writing of history in general and on English and British history in particular. This orientation requires that we think about the effects of racism both in its relationship to nationalism and in relation to the nationalist historiography produced by both radical and conservative historians.

I want, then, to speak as a representative of a diverse body of work, loosely both historical and sociological, which has pointed to the salience of 'race' as a structuring feature of British society and drawn attention to some of the new varieties of racist discourse and racial politics found in this country during the last twenty years.[1] An emphasis on culture lends this novel racial thinking its primary distinguishing characteristic. The term 'culture' has expanded to displace any overt references to 'race' in the older, biological sense of the term. Culture is reductively

This chapter was a talk given at a conference on the National Curriculum for History, hosted by History Workshop at Ruskin College. It was published in *History Workshop* in 1990.

conceived and is always primarily and 'naturally' reproduced in families. The nation is, in turn, conceived as a neat, symmetrical accumulation of family units and the supposedly homogenous culture – secured in part by sustained exposure to national history in the classroom – culminates in the experience of unified and continuous national identity. It would appear that historians are being entrusted with the precious task of making and reproducing a national identity which is frequently presented as beleaguered and fragile. The proposed role of history teaching in the transmission of this authentic national culture reveals the confluence of 'race', nationality and culture in the contemporary politics of racial exclusion. The same fixation with cultural difference has also enabled this reasonable racism to escape the conventional designation of politics into left and right and, of course, to evade the idea of race as hierarchy in favour of a pseudo-pluralism which is only betrayed in the end by its steely lack of tolerance.[2]

As part of a broad political commitment to the black settler populations of this country, a number of us, black and white, have been trying to explore what happens when this new racism brings 'race' and nation very closely together. The characteristic outcome is a situation in which blackness appears as a kind of disqualification from membership of the national community: the same national community which will be celebrated and reproduced in the reformed pedagogy of national history. The relationship between racism and nationalism has also emerged as the mainspring of a populist politics, bolstered by debates around immigration, crime, religion and, increasingly, the educational proclivities of the minority ethnic population. The 'Asian' preference for single-sex education for Muslim girls and the Caribbean longing for the authoritarian regimes of Victorian-style schooling are familiar themes here. These and other recent conflicts in and around educational institutions in this country suggest that if these forms of racism are to be effectively opposed, some innovative political strategies will have to be devised, strategies that can answer this preoccupation with culture directly with a new language of cultural democracy. This crisis of cultural difference, cultural relativism and cultural value,[3] which frames current debates over *The Satanic Verses*, is the essential background to our meeting this morning.

Unfortunately, the language of anti-racist political struggle has been so discredited – not least by its moralistic misuse in the context of educational institutions[4] – that we are obliged to find new ways of elaborating our critique of educational practices and of rethinking the relationship between race, nation and ethnic identities. In my view, one tentative step forward lies in seeing the new culturalist racism as but one example of what might be called ethnic absolutism. This is a reductive, essentialist understanding of ethnic and national difference which operates through an absolute sense of culture so powerful that it is capable of separating people off from each other and diverting them into social and historical locations that are understood to be mutually impermeable and incommensurable. Ethnic absolutism may not trade in the vocabularies of 'race'. It may be remote from the symbolism of colour and, most important of all, it can afflict anyone. In fact, those who experience racism themselves may be particularly prone to its lure. They often seize its simple, self-evident truths as a way of rationalizing their subordination and comprehending their own particularity. It is therefore necessary to argue against the rhetoric of cultural insiderism[5] and the narrow practice of cultural nationalism, whatever their source.

In my own work, I have become increasingly fascinated by the way in which black nationalism developed in the nineteenth century.[6] It would seem that black nationalism is also bound by its origins in Romantic theories of the nation and nation-building. Edward Wilmot Blyden, Martin Delany, Alexander Crummell,

James Theodore Holly and the rest of the intelligentsia of the black Atlantic world were, to varying degrees, indebted to the nationalist thinking of Herder, Schleiermacher, Hegel and von Treitschke. W. E. B. Du Bois, who studied under Treitschke in Berlin, went so far as to make Bismarck the subject of his graduation address from Fisk University in 1888. Reflecting on this years later in *Dusk of Dawn*, he wrote:

> Bismarck was my hero. He made a nation out of a mass of bickering peoples. He had dominated the whole development with his strength until he crowned an emperor at Versailles. This foreshadowed in my mind the kind of thing that American Negroes must do, marching forward with strength and determination under trained leadership.[7]

This model of national development has a special appeal to the 'bickering peoples' of the black Atlantic diaspora and inspired their efforts to construct a nation-state on African soil. But there are other, even more pernicious, varieties of nationalism which have been elaborated from radical and even socialist sources. Here it is important for us to focus on the very specific forms of English cultural nationalism that can be used to illustrate an important convergence between the New Right and the New Left around the meaning of national tradition and ethnic identity. I still hold to the view that a great deal of New Left historiography is articulated in an explicitly nationalistic register.[8] Whether History Workshop is legitimately or illegitimately descended from this perspective remains to be worked out. Certainly the great power and authority of the New Left historians should not lead us to overlook the way in which their work hosts an encounter between the intellectual and political legacies of socialism in one country and a different, rather volkish, tradition of national popular radicalism seemingly transmitted with only minor interruptions from Putney Heath to Greenham Common. There is a great deal more to say about this left nationalism and the statist conceptions of political change that bolster it. The aspiration to produce a popular culture which the left can somehow orchestrate or even command is understandable, although the doggedly ethnocentric character of these desires is perplexing. In a situation where 'race', nation, culture and ethnicity are used almost as synonyms, the very best that can be said about it is that it is ambiguous as far as the politics of racism are concerned. If we turn to the historiography of this country, this nativistic impulse represents a great intellectual weakness. The language of national belonging and patriotism has acquired a series of racial referents that cannot be spontaneously dislodged by a pure act of will. They will not necessarily go away if we opt to overlook them. They may recede and lose their power while new conceptions of locality and connectedness emerge, but ethnocentrism[9] may be enhanced amidst the cultural order of a new Europe in which chauvinistic concern with ethnic particularity has been rehabilitated even as the political and economic integration of nation-states proceeds. Beyond the parochial boundaries of British political life, the idea that identity and culture are exclusively *national* phenomena, and the related notion that unchanging essences of ethnic or national distinctiveness are automatically, though mysteriously, produced from their own guts, have come to constitute a major political problem. These ideas can be effectively counterposed to the forms of identity and struggle developed – of necessity – by dispersed peoples for whom nationality, ethnicity and the nation-state are perhaps not so tightly associated and for whom the condition of exile becomes a privilege rather than a handicap.

This is a roundabout way of saying why I do not accept the polarization implicit in the title of this morning's session: 'National History, for and against'. I will be bolder than that and say that I am tired of the dualistic thinking that risks attempting to reduce the world to a set of theoretical categories and is such a recurrent feature of the drive towards simplicity which so often unravels both anti-racism and internationalism. This approach says that you are either for or against the nation, for blacks and against whites. It says that in the operation of racism there are only ever two great camps: the victims and the perpetrators, as if the fixity and coherence of these complex terms and positions can be readily and permanently established. Apart from the way that this binary division abolishes the space and the opportunity for anti-racist intervention, it is important to remember that as historians we have to be concerned about the witnesses too. I think we need a new line of thought that goes beyond 'either/or-ism' into a different conceptual logic of supplementarity. In its simplest form, this might turn on the alternative couplet 'both/and'. I make no apology for the fact that this shift in my own thinking arises from a desire to be recognized as being both black and English in addition to everything else that I am.

It is not, then, a matter of being either for or against national history. Somewhere between the local and the global there must be a place for that nation-state and indeed for the myths and dreams of national or ethnic collectivity that condition our political predicament even as the relationship between the local and the global is itself transformed. The first question I would ask you to consider is therefore to be reformulated thus: what value should we attach to the claims which nationality makes when we weigh them against the other political and theoretical options we encounter in the writing of history? Here I have found it useful to return to Gramsci's idea of a critical self-inventory. He says:

> The starting-point of critical elaboration is the consciousness of what one really is, and is 'knowing thyself' as a product of the historical process to date which has deposited in you an

> *infinity of traces, without leaving an inventory.*[10] (my
> emphasis)

There are all sorts of reasons that, as the era of nation-states
promises to draw to a close, the nation should not be accepted as
the principal means to organize that inventory, if indeed that
inventory can be organized at all. The nation should have no
special privileges in the process of its production and enjoy no
immunity from prosecution. Looking at the contemporary
growth of supra-national structures of domination and control
in both economic and political life prompts further questions for
me about the ways in which historians have dealt with the modes
of production, social movements and patterns of informational
exchange in the past which have criss-crossed national boundaries. How do we explain the apparent monopoly of the nation-
state as an intermediate category lodged between the local and
the global? C. L. R. James, whose extraordinary life bears witness to the intellectual privileges that flow from movement and
lack of fixity, provides a general warning in *Notes on Dialectics*
which may be of value here:

> Now one of the chief errors of thought is to continue to think
> in one set of forms, categories, ideas, etc., when the object,
> the content, has moved on, has created or laid premises for an
> extension, a development of thought.[11]

In the light of James's injunction, it seems worthwhile to consider the possibility that the borders of the nation may represent
a rather arbitrary point at which to pause in our efforts to comprehend the past. I want to ask you whether you think that we
cling to the nation all the more tightly because the order of
certainty with which it is associated is currently being torn away.
I want to direct our discussion towards the ways in which

writing merely national histories may now be inadequate. It may still be necessary but it is certainly insufficient. There was fleeting recognition of this in the paper that Raphael Samuel circulated prior to this session. But I want to say in response to him that I do not think he can have it both ways. If the national question is going to be allowed to implode, as he seemed to suggest in the latter parts of that document, we should be more open about our desire to see the back of it. We cannot plausibly enthrone the idea of national history while simultaneously seeking to take it, and all it symbolizes, apart. Raphael maintains this contradictory position only at the price of a telling silence over the fate of political nationalism. What transpires in the history classroom is, after all, overdetermined by the populist political nationalism I have already mentioned. This imposes significant constraints on voluntaristic attempts to re-configure national identity in a more pluralistic manner, however well intentioned they may be.

If we cannot proceed simply by either claiming the nation as our own or by revealing its internal differentiation as well as its imperial and militaristic legacies, what are we to do? It is clear that we cannot deal with the problem by seeking to add 'Empire' into a pre-existing syllabus or by tacking on the supposedly discrete and distinct histories of 'minority' groups whose silenced and invisible presences can be shown to be dictating the hidden pattern of British national identity in the modern world. Rather than clinging to the idea of nation as the central means to organize our thoughts about the past, I would like to see us trying to be a little bit more imaginative. There are, for example, grounds on which we can defend the vitality and richness of what might be called 'webbed accounts'[12] in contrast with the static and arid state of historiography's master narratives. These accounts might strive to transcend national boundaries and would reveal the conspicuous internal differentiation of national communities. Their intellectual restlessness might also endeavour to make a virtue out of the inescapable partiality of perspective on which they are premised, and which helps to locate the distinctive travelling standpoint from which they evaluate the turbulence and radical contingency of modern social life. This assumes a far more refined politics of location than that currently allowed by the desperate cartography of nation-states.

This proposal would involve rewriting British history to the point at which it ceases to be recognizably British at all. Pointers towards how this might be done already exist. Here, I want to emphasize the decidedly transnational character of modes of production, social movements and informational exchanges. In work that I have been doing recently on the travels of black abolitionists in the nineteenth century, I have been struck by something prefigurative, which indicates that by acting locally and thinking globally in their struggles against slavery and racial domination, these movements have something to teach us today. The work of historians like Peter Linebaugh[13] and Marcus Rediker,[14] who have abrogated nationalism in favour of an Atlantic perspective on the eighteenth century, has also been particularly inspiring. It is no accident that this work has its origins outside Britain. Linebaugh actually offers an appropriate metaphor when he writes of the moribund categories of merely national history endeavouring to bury the vitality of political movements in so many ethnically and economistically arranged cemetery plots.

My own interest in these problems derives from the example offered by the history of the black Atlantic world. It contains a fluid and dynamic cultural system that escapes the grasp of nation-states and national conceptions of political and economic development. The writers and political thinkers generated within the black Atlantic tradition have produced a rich body of work in which reflection on nationality, hybridity, independence, syncretism and self-determination have been acknowledged as central political and philosophical questions for something like 200 years. There is something exemplary in that work and it remains a profound intellectual and political resource for *whoever* seeks it out and makes use of it.

To sum up then, I am not against the nation (we have to put it somewhere) but the term 'national history' seems to open the door to nationalism. Those who are content to produce merely national histories should be able to get on with their work. I repeat that what I am concerned with is the historiography of ethnic absolutism. I am against the rhetoric of cultural insiderism, whatever its source, because I think it is too readily linked to unacceptable ideas of homogenous national culture and exclusionary national or ethnic belonging. There is, of course, no necessary connection here with any ideas about 'race'.

Notes

1. A random selection of texts here might include Peter Fryer, *Staying Power: The History of Black People in Britain*, Pluto, London, 1984; Peter Fryer, *Black People in the British Empire*, Pluto, London, 1988; Stuart Hall et al, *Policing the Crisis*, Macmillan, London, 1978; John MacKenzie (ed.), *Imperialism and Popular Culture*, Manchester University Press, 1986; Edward Pilkington, *Beyond the Mother Country*, I. B. Tauris, London, 1988; Ron Ramdin, *The Making of the Black Working Class in Britain*, Gower, London, 1987; Robin Blackburn, *The Overthrow of Colonial Slavery, 1766–1848*, Verso, London, 1988.

2. Fay Weldon, *Sacred Cows*, Chatto & Windus (Counterblast pamphlet), London, 1989.

3. Barbara Herrnstein Smith, *Contingencies of Value*, Harvard University Press, 1988.

4. Ian MacDonald, R. Bhavnani, L. Khan and A. John, *Murder in the Playground*, Longsight Press, London, 1989.

5. Werner Sollors, *Beyond Ethnicity: Consent and Descent in American Culture*, Oxford University Press, 1986.

6. Immanuel Geiss, *The Pan-African Movement*, Methuen, London, 1974; Wilson Moses, *The Golden Age of Black Nationalism*, Oxford University Press, 1978.

7. W. E. B. Du Bois, *Dusk of Dawn* (1940), Viking, New York, 1986, p. 577

8. Vron Ware, 'The Good, the Bad and the Foolhardy: Moving the frontiers of British women's history', in F. Røgilds (ed.), *Every Cloud Has a Silver Lining: Lectures on Everyday Life, Cultural Production and Race*, Akademisk Forlag, London, 1990.

9. V. Y. Mudimbe, *The Invention of Africa*, Indiana University Press/James Currey, 1988.

10. Antonio Gramsci, 'The Study of Philosophy', in *Selections from Prison Notebooks*, Lawrence & Wishart, London, 1971, p. 324.

11. C. L. R. James, *Notes on Dialectics*, Allison & Busby, London, 1980, p. 15.

12. Donna Haraway, 'Situated Knowledges: the science question in feminism and the privilege of partial perspective', *Feminist Studies*, vol. 14, no. 3, Fall 1988.

13. Peter Linebaugh, 'All the Atlantic Mountains Shook', *Labour/Le Travailleur*, vol. 10, 1982.

14. Marcus Rediker, *Between the Devil and the Deep Blue Sea*, Cambridge University Press, 1988.

4   Art of darkness

*Black art and the problem
of belonging to England*

The politics of race has changed. The idea of a narrow
anti-racism, for example, is no longer tenable. This situation has
not come about because racism is less pernicious or because the
long-term goal of racial justice is any less worthy. This change is
not a result of the political ineptitude of anti-racist work in local
authorities, or of the trivialization of black life which often characterized that work, nor even of the way that the idea of anti-
racism has itself been dragged through the mud by moralism and
discredited yet further by the excesses of its evangelical cadres.
None of these noxious features announces the end of anti-racism
as we have known it. It is the issue of culture and the failings
of anti-racist practice to deal effectively with the cultural
dimensions of racial politics in this country that confirm its
redundancy.

Well before *The Satanic Verses* underscored this critical defi-
ciency, organized anti-racism had been unable to respond to the
varieties of racist discourse that linked understanding of race to
cultural difference rather than biological hierarchy. Anti-
racism was confidently able to define racism in the sum of prejudice and power but could not define race apart from the cultural

A shorter version of this chapter was published in *The New Statesman* in 1990.

characteristics which sometimes give 'racial' groups their cohesion. Anti-racism could not theorize the relationship between 'race' and culture because these two ideas were not effectively distinguished. Anti-racists colluded with their New Right opponents by reducing the former to the latter. They remained inert while ideas of race and nation became ever more closely associated in a new popular, patriotic brew. Their own covert reliance on ethnic absolutes made it hard to deny coherently the legitimacy of ethnic absolutism when it appeared in the Honeyford brand of reasoned British nativism.

In this climate, to be both black and British was thought to be an impossibly compound identity. To be British is, in any case, to contract into a category of administrative convenience rather than an ethnic identity. It's an ambiguous word which often refuses it's own obvious cultural referents. The term 'English', which is often mistakenly substituted for it, acts as a partial and manifestly inadequate cultural counterpart. The disjuncture between the two terms is a continual reminder not just of English dominance over Scots, Welsh and Irish people, but also that a British state can exist comfortably without the benefit of a unified British culture. The idea of an authentic cultural content of our national life is therefore constructed through an appeal to Englishness rather than Britishness. It is around this concept that the difficult tasks of creating a more pluralistic sense of national identity and a new conception of national culture revolve.

These problems have a special significance for the artists of Britain's emergent black vernacular. They echo through musician Jazzie B.'s boast that he is proud to be both black and English and even resound when Ian Wright, the national B-team striker, confides to the *Daily Star* that he weeps as he pulls on his white England shirt. There is, however, no more striking example of the manner in which these vital conflicts are resolved by blacks in this country than painter Sonia Boyce's ironic re-figuration of herself in the guise of an English rose. All these actions are part of a wider cultural struggle to affiliate with England and, in so doing, to change what it means to be English. These young, gifted and black Britons are not naive. The impact of a diaspora sensibility on their lives means that they can readily comprehend the limitations of national identities as such. Contemporary racism forces the most sensitive of them to try to understand the enduring appeal of national belonging. Their tentative but nonetheless insubordinate gestures signify an approach that has moved far beyond the typical anti-racist practice of peering into the murky pool of English culture in order to locate evidence of its monolithically racist character. The desire to make art out of being both black and English has become a major issue in the black art movement and should be seen as part of the long, micro-political task of recoding the cultural core of national life. In this light, the fissures, stress cracks and structural fatigue in the edifices of Englishness become more interesting and acquire their own beauty. With ethnic absolutism left behind, the tasks of demolition and reconstruction may also provide an opportunity to create a division of political labour in which white radicals can share.

The burgeoning musical distinctiveness of black England has provided the easiest means to explore this process of cultural exchange and transformation. However, during the 1980s the movement of black artists encompassed a variety of other expressive forms. The recent exhibition at the Hayward Gallery in which Sonia Boyce's picture is featured has provided an overdue occasion to reflect on the development of black visual arts, the distinct place they occupy in the art establishment and their importance for the black communities. This exhibition – 'The Other Story' – has also performed the valuable role of flushing out the ethnocentric attitudes of a number of critics who have secreted the discourse of white supremacy in their commentaries on the show. Visual art currently constitutes a significant battle-ground because aesthetic issues are particularly close to the surface of individual judgements and, above all, because the majority of its critics are bound by the common-sense view that good art is universally recognizable and cultural background is not a factor either in its production or its appreciation. This position has remained largely unaffected by any relativist fall-out from anti-racist orthodoxy.

It is important to appreciate that the idea of universality on which aesthetic judgements depend was itself constructed out of debates in which racial difference was a central issue. In Hegel's influential work, for example, blacks were incorporated directly into the discussion of aesthetics.[1] The capacity to make art was identified as a sign of the progress of non-Europeans out of their prehistoric state and into both history and culture. Writing before scientific racism gained its intellectual grip, Hegel identi-fied the major difference between blacks and whites as a cultural or perceptual one. He denied blacks the ability to appreciate the necessary mystery involved in the creation of truly symbolic art and placed them outside the realm of authentic aesthetic sensi-bility. Unlike the American Indians whom he saw as effectively destroyed by the exposure to the culture and values of the West, he endowed blacks with the potential to progress into culture even if they were often viewed as a childlike group that could perceive higher values but was incapable of objectifying them as artistic abstractions. Where these higher values were perceived, the childlike blacks transferred 'them to the next best stone, which they thus make their fetish'.[2] Blacks perceive the divine objects they have created as sublime, but Europeans see them as 'hideous' just as they hear non-European music as 'the most detestable noise'.

The distinctively English idioms of art criticism also rest on aesthetic principles produced during a period when slavery was still part of western civilization and therefore a fundamentally political concept. Here too, the image of the black played an important role in debates over taste, judgement and the role of culturally specific experience in grounding aesthetic principles. Burke's discussion of the sublime is striking for its association of darkness with the 'blackness' of a black woman's skin. Some of the reviews of the Hayward exhibition suggest that assimilating the work of black artists to a concept of the primitive, and declaring it bad modern art on that basis, is an enduring strategy. In his catalogue the show's curator, Rashid Araeen, counters it by arguing that it is necessary to rewrite the history of modern art. This is to be achieved mainly through a tried and tested anti-racist approach: black creativity has been excluded from the aesthetic citadels of modernity and post-modernity and this wrong can be redressed by the corrective reconstruction of the Western canon. No doubt there are many good reasons for this to be done. Successive generations of black artists have suffered from the contempt and hostility of critics, galleries and potential patrons. But if this process of rewriting art history along multi-cultural lines is not to degenerate into a crude debate over who did what first, there are significant problems to be faced. The first of these is the need to produce new concepts and a *non-narrative* periodization of Western art. Despite its title, 'The Other Story' is an important contribution to this long-term task.

The necessary but insufficient tactic of corrective inclusion that Araeen advocates leaves dominant notions of art and artistic creativity entirely unscathed. Furthermore, it attempts to force a wide range of post-colonial and non-European art practice into the rigid sequence that leads from modernism to post-modernism. This is not always possible, let alone desirable. Most importantly, this approach seems to accept the idea that 'race' is something that enters English culture from the outside during the post-war period. It shrinks before the wider obligation to adapt and transform understanding of English culture as a whole so that being black and English is no longer either a curiosity or an outrage. Araeen appreciates that the mere existence of black artists in the West challenges art history's sense of where the modern begins, let alone its line between the modern and the post-modern, but his argument remains somehow too internal to the institutional world of art. Perhaps moving outside it would expose the enormous generational and political differences between the artists who contributed to 'The Other Story'.

Black artists are now in a position to attempt a more ambitious project than simply filling in the spaces that racism has left blank in the history of art. They are already working to re-compose understanding of English culture, and their creativity needs to be complemented by a re-reading of that culture's history which places the idea of 'race' at the centre rather than the margin. The visual arts will play a key role in this, not just because of the tremendous vitality of the black fine art during the last decade, but because architecture, aesthetics and art have recently re-emerged as politically significant issues. As the principal public means to mark out and signify the cultural limits of national life, they will have a direct bearing on what the cultural order of a new Europe will be.

An editorial in a recent issue of the journal *Modern Painters*,[3] which pleaded for Prince Charles to extend his well-known ideas about architecture into a discussion of art, offered an important insight into this. Though sometimes cited as evidence of his eccentricity, Charles's interest in his black subjects-to-be is well known. These views should not, however, distract us from the less wholesome ways in which some of his supporters would link the relationship between what is national and what is natural in a political discourse which offers the black English very little. The newer, culturally focused varieties of racism I have described make no appeal whatsoever to biology but they view the nation as a *natural* unit formed spontaneously from the association of families. The national frontier around authentic English culture marks the boundaries of the national community as naturally and as finally as the white cliffs of Dover.

The *Modern Painters* editorial identified the things 'for which the Prince has so eloquently argued' as 'the replenishment of traditional skills, a renewed sense of the spiritual dimensions of aesthetic life' and 'imaginative involvement with the natural landscape'. These great themes were given a narrowly national currency and linked to 'the historic achievements of the British School'. There are plenty of clues here that we are dealing with a notion of national culture that is as homogeneous as it is ethnically undifferentiated. It becomes necessary to ask whether the aesthetic that underlies these suggestions would view blacks as a natural and acceptable presence in the English landscapes it reveres? The black presence in cities is novel and symptomatic of their post-war decline but it is somehow appropriate. Contemporary racism has identified black settlers with the cities in which most of them live and their cultural distinctiveness with its urban setting. Black life discovered amidst urban chaos and squalor has contributed new images of dangerousness and hedonism to the anti-urbanism of much English cultural commentary. How much less congruent is a black presence with the natural landscapes within which historically authentic English sensibility has been formed?

Here, the issue of black settlement needs to be separated from consideration of how blacks have been pictured in England's own imagination. The imagery of race has a much longer lineage in English cultural life than the aura of post-war novelty allows us to see. The theme of racial difference has also been extensively addressed from within that tradition. It should not be surprising that the relationship between the forces of nature and the human processes that culminate in racial exploitation has been explored before. It can even be found in what the editors of *Modern Painters* would probably regard as the exalted point in the artistic inventory of English national culture represented by John Ruskin and his first mentor, J. M. W. Turner.

Turner's famous tragic picture 'Slavers Throwing Overboard the Dead and Dying: Typhoon coming on' (also known as 'The Slave Ship') draws these strands together. The picture deploys the imagery of wrathful nature and of dying slaves as powerful means to highlight the degenerate and irrational nature of English civil society as it entered the 1840s. This work can provide a small illustration both of the extent to which race has been tacitly erased from discussion of English culture and how a 'racial' theme, relocated at the heart of national self-understanding, can contribute to a new more pluralistic conceptualization of both England and Britain.

Turner and Ruskin, who owned 'The Slave Ship' for twenty-eight years, currently enjoy special status in contemporary cultural life. Turner is a leading player in the unfolding drama of our national heritage, while Ruskin's social thought was an important inspiration in the development of New Left thinking about English intellectual history. More recently, his aesthetic ideas have supplied the raw material for precisely the ambiguous, organicist conception of English culture celebrated in the reborn *Modern Painters* and its royalist editorial. Turner's picture was first publicly shown in London in 1840, a few weeks before the World Anti-slavery Convention met in the Strand's Exeter Hall. Its immediate inspiration seems to have been James Thomson's poem 'The Seasons', although it may also have been inspired by Thomas Clarkson's accounts of barbaric events aboard the slave ships *Zong* and *Rodeur*. The artist's apparent alignment with the abolitionist cause has been queried by some commentators, but the lines which accompanied the painting illuminate his elemental despair for which the morality of the traffic in slaves offered a striking and appropriate symbol: 'hope hope fallacious hope where is thy market now?'

The picture was not well received, opinion being divided as to whether it was absurd rather than sublime. *The Times* ridiculed it and drew attention to 'the leg of a negro, which is about to afford a nibble to a John Dory, a pair of soles and a shoal of whitebait'. Writing in *Fraser's Magazine* Thackeray was not slow to query the use to which the images of the trade had been put:

> the slaver throwing its cargo overboard is the most tremendous piece of colour that ever was seen . . . The sun glares down upon a horrible sea of emerald and purple, into which chocolate coloured slaves are plunged, and chains that will not sink; and round these are floundering such a race of fishes as was never seen in the saeculum Pyrrhae . . . horrid spreading polypi, like huge, slimy, poached eggs, in which hapless niggers, plunge and disappear. Ye gods what a 'middle passage'!

Ruskin's father gave him the picture in January 1844 as a New Year's present to celebrate the publication of the first volume of the original *Modern Painters*. An entry in his diary a couple of days before the painting was delivered conveys his excitement and something of his early responses to the picture:

> Suspense about Slaver. My heart is all on eyes of *fish* now – it knew something of other kind of eyes once, and of slavery too, in its way. Its slavery now is colder like being bound to the dead, as in old Spanish cruelty.[4]

These private acknowledgements of the metaphysical potency of the painting's theme contrast quite sharply with the famous description of the painting he had penned previously for *Modern*

Painters.[5] Here, Ruskin's evaluation of the painting forms part of his discussion of how water should be painted. He praised Turner's picture because it includes 'the noblest sea that Turner has ever painted' which is also 'the noblest certainly ever painted by man'. He continues: 'if I were reduced to rest Turner's immortality upon any single work, I should choose this'. The celebrated passage is too long to be quoted here but it is significant that Ruskin relegates the information that 'the guilty ship', 'girded with condemnation', is a slaver, to an extraordinary footnote: 'she is a slaver, throwing her slaves overboard. The near sea is encumbered with corpses.' One of Ruskin's biographers tells us that William Morris, Burne-Jones and other members of their set at Oxford were so deeply moved by the 'weltering oceans of eloquence' found in Ruskin's description of the ship that Morris would 'chant' the passage in his mighty singing voice. We are not told if the crucial footnote featured in these dramatic presentations.[6] It seems legitimate to draw attention to Ruskin's inability to integrate his aesthetic commentary on the painting with an open acknowledgement of its 'racial' content. Why was the 'racial' theme, which contributes directly to the conspicuous power of the work, given no aesthetic significance of its own? Three years after his notorious involvement in the campaign to defend Governor Eyre's brutal handling of the Morant Bay rebellion in Jamaica, Ruskin put the painting up for sale at Christie's. It is said that he had begun to find the subject matter of his father's gift too painful to live with. No buyer was found at that time and he eventually sold the picture to an American three years later. The painting has remained in the United States ever since and is now exhibited at the Museum of Fine Arts in Boston. Its exile also raises significant questions for the cultural historian as to the apparently un-English nature of its content.

It would be simplistic, even absurd, to characterize any of the complex exchanges around Turner's extraordinary painting as racist in the modern sense of the term. It is exciting to discover how the imagery of race and slavery appears centrally in Victorian debates over what England had been and what it was to become. The painting offers one opportunity to appreciate that English art and aesthetics are not simply in place alongside English thinking about race. Thinking about England is being conducted through the 'racial' symbolism that artistic images of black suffering provide. These images were not an alien or unnatural presence that had somehow intruded into English life from the outside. They were an integral means with which England was able to make sense of itself and its destiny.

The picture and its strange history pose a challenge to the black English today. It demands that we strive to integrate the different dimensions of our hybrid cultural heritage more effectively. If we are to change England by being English in addition to everything else that we are, our reflections on it and other comparable controversies in national art and letters must be synthesized with the different agenda of difficulties that emerges from our need to comprehend a phenomenon like the Hayward exhibition and the movement that produced it. In doing this, we may discover that our story is not the *other* story after all but *the* story of England in the modern world. The main danger we face in embarking on this difficult course is that these divergent political and aesthetic commentaries will remain the exclusive property of two mutually opposed definitions of cultural nationalism: one black, one white. Each has its own mystical sense of the relationship between blood, soil and seawater. Neither of them offers anything constructive for the future.

Notes

1. Sander Gilman. 'The Figure of the Black in German Aesthetic Theory', *Eighteenth Century Studies*, vol 8, 1975, pp. 373–91.
2. See the discussion of the fetish in the section on the geographical basis of history which introduces Hegel's lectures on *The Philosophy of History*, Dover, New York, 1956, pp. 91–9.
3. *Modern Painters*, vol. 2, no. 3, Autumn 1989.
4. *Diaries of John Ruskin*, ed. Joan Evans and J. H. Whitehouse, entry for 27 December 1843. Clarendon Press, Oxford, 1956.
5. Vol. 1 section 5, ch. III, section 39.
6. E. T. Cook, *Life of Ruskin*, 2 vols, George Allen, London, 1911, p. 147.

5 Frank Bruno or Salman Rushdie?

Frank Bruno has become a significant public figure, an unlikely but nonetheless important symbol of the future of blacks in this country. His defeat by Mike Tyson drew no serious comment from cultural critics or commentators. Yet over 14 million Britons watched the first showing of that contest which turned out to be the most popular sporting event of the decade. The adulation heaped on Frank is unprecedented for a black athlete, unmatched even by the praise showered on Daley Thompson at the peak of his career or on Tessa Sanderson before she fell foul of her rival Fatima Whitbread. In tasting defeat, Frank found a triumph which had considerable significance beyond the sporting sub-culture in which it originated. This came across in the extraordinary way that Frank Bruno instantly became 'our Frank': a broad English oak, standing sluggish if not firm, amidst the unwholesome tornado of Tyson's Bedford Stuyvesant atavism.

England's other pre-eminent black sportsman, John Barnes, provides an interesting comparison. Barnes retains a Jamaican passport and remains an enigmatic and peripheral figure, drifting aimlessly on the wing of national life. His role in the team mirrors

A shorter version of this chapter was published in *The New Statesman* in 1990.

the problems of his public personality and, in spite of his heroic and dignified behaviour in the aftermath of the Hillsborough tragedy, he seems unlikely ever to get stuck into the hard graft involved in being British. In contrast, Frank's sincere patriotism and cultural authenticity are self-evident. His canonization was particularly important because it happened at a time when racism regularly constructed blackness and Britishness as mutually exclusive social and cultural categories. The key to comprehending his special significance lies first in his obvious Englishness – an attribute which has been noted by several commentators but not explored. He was, for example, casually compared to St George by one writer and ridiculed by another who suggested that it would have been more appropriate for him to have fought the all-conquering world champion wearing a red nose. These sniggery responses, which view Frank as a kind of Gary Wilmot in Lonsdale trimmings, typify a peculiar malaise that takes hold of English critical thinking where race is concerned. An additional symptom of this is the inability to appreciate how both racialized subjectivity and the national identity that nourishes it have been crucially shaped by the discourses of sporting achievement in popular culture and beyond. It is hard to avoid the conclusion that the inability to see Frank as a significant symbol, or indeed, to see Frank at all, is a striking illustration of the remoteness and introspection that characterize so much commentary on popular culture.

If the radicals and the anti-racists either ignored or ridiculed Frank, those who did notice him – on the right and in the tabloid press – elected to celebrate his performance, seeing in it a deep cultural affiliation to the British national community. It was his predictable failure that cogently expressed all that community's sterling masculine qualities. Failure became heroic rather than disappointing and was rapidly annexed by the 'Eddie the Eagle' syndrome whereby English losers are able to transcend the indignity of defeat and acquire special status. You can just imagine the over-wordy, red, white and blue T-shirts 'Two world wars, one World Cup and eight failed attempts at the World Heavyweight Championship'.

The broader resonance of Frank's heroism of the vanquished and conspicuous 'trans-racial' popularity for the cultural dimensions of racism and nationalism in this country should have been obvious at any time. But coming in the midst of the Rushdie affair, its important lessons should have appeared all the more striking. Frank's physical accomplishment, however meagre beside Tyson's own, conveys a clear message that *some* representatives of the ethnic minorities in this country *are* capable and willing to make the cultural and social adaptations demanded of them in the wake of *The Satanic Verses*. For a while, Frank's muscular black English masculinity became a counterpart to the esoteric and scholastic image of Rushdie – the middle-class intellectual *immigrant* – so remote from the world of ordinary folk that he was able to misjudge it so tragically.

For two weeks the two stories were articulated directly together. They fed off each other, echoing, replying and re-working the same range of visceral themes: belonging and exclusion, sameness and assimilation, the difficulty of escaping from the racial cultures which now more than ever appeared to constitute an absolute division in history and humanity.

It is tempting to suggest that the inability to perceive the connection between these two narratives of black cultural development itself portrays the weakness of the left/liberal line within the *Satanic Verses* debate. Alongside the lofty principles and abstract aesthetic excellence invoked by Rushdie's supporters in the nation's literary elite, Frank's triumph must appear trivial and base. But, every bit as much as the responses to Rushdie's book, Frank's five stumbling rounds in Vegas offered a means to clarify contemporary British identity and values. The image of each man stood as a convenient emblem for one of Britain's black settler communities, marking out their respective rates of progress towards integration. Each image increased its symbolic power through implicit references to the other – its precise inversion. The same complex interplay was to be repeated exactly one year later when Frank's wedding to his long-time sweetheart coincided with the anniversary of Ayatollah Khomeini's fatwa.

The different ways in which the class and the masculinity of both men worked to portray wider ideas of race and national identity needs to be located in the context of the historic folk grammar of British racism. This in turn requires consideration of what has been called the 'Goldilocks-and-the-three-bears theory of racial culture and identity'. This common-sense perspective specifies that animal blacks enjoy an excess of brute physicality and wily oriental gentlemen conversely display a surfeit of cerebral power, while only the authentic Anglo-Brit is able to luxuriate in the perfect equilibrium of body and mind.

The right, of course, had no difficulty in recognizing the manner in which Bruno had become important or the obvious relationship between the parallel ordeals of Bruno and Rushdie. This tale of two immigrants was immediately perceived as one epic account of the progress of Britain's black settlers. In *The Sunday Telegraph* Walter Ellis outlined the peculiar mechanisms whereby, in losing his big fight, Big Frank had ironically won the hearts of the nation:

> What we admire about him is his defiant dignity in the face of impending calamity . . . When Frank turned up in a Savile Row suit for a prefight news conference and Tyson appeared in what looked like an outsize babygrow, the writing was already on the wall . . .

In a direct comparison with Rushdie, Ellis concluded that being British was what Big Frank did best: 'In the area of Englishness he is tops, the champ, the number one man.' Frank's well-publicized depression at having let the British public down was the cherry on a patriotic cake.

The black prizefighter has a long and noble history in this country and an almost unbroken line of black pugilists connects Frank's recent modest efforts to the brave strivings of Joe Leashley in 1791. Pierce Egan's *Boxiana,* first published in 1812, is replete with tales of Frank's nineteenth-century antecedents. Though probably more nimble than Bruno, the most famous of these men, Bill Richmond, was similarly well-dressed and smart. Richmond was landlord of the Horse and Dolphin pub near Leicester Square and is probably best remembered for having taught William Hazlitt to use his fists. Comparing Richmond to Othello, Egan continues: 'we cannot omit stating of our hero that he is intelligent, communicative, and well behaved'. We are also informed that, notwithstanding a defect in one of his knees, Mr Richmond excelled as a cricketer.

It becomes necessary to ask how the long-overdue entry of a black boxer into the mystical communion of authentic British nationality has been achieved. The obvious answer lies in the nature of the sport in which 'our Frank' has chosen to earn his corn. The heavyweight division is absolutely unmatched as a location for putting masculine aggression on display. But, apart from the simple fact that he is a boxer, Frank has considerable charm and can be witty, even if his 'suntan' gag has been seriously over-used. He toys cleverly with the white audience's expectation that he is nothing more than a punch-drunk buffoon. He wears his Savile Row suits with grace and a genuine humility shines like a beacon through the hype that surrounds him. It is only half a joke to say that Frank has been given a halo. In him, the gentle giant and the noble savage fuse to form a black man who cares so little for his beefcake profile that he cries in public – no wonder Iron Mike walked all over him.

Frank's class, and particularly his South London working-class speech, is another powerful factor. It provides a clue to the construction of his own ethnicity in the circuitous route from Wandsworth to Essex via the Old Kent Road. At the most basic level, his class tells us that he is one of the boys. His definition of manliness works through the imagery and symbols of class as well as those of race. What makes him heroic works both in spite of his blackness *and* because of it. The extraordinary detail with which his personal history has been revealed in the media is a further means to place him. We now know, for example, that a kindly school-dinner lady gave him extra puddings to help him on his way. We know that his mother sits in the toilet rather than watch her boy in combat. We know how his sister Angela was mistakenly manhandled by security guards. We know above all about Frank's partner, Laura, and their two daughters, Nicola (6) and Rachel (2) – the two tiny knockouts who wait to welcome him home to Hornchurch. It is not only that the issue of whether Frank would finally make an honest woman of Laura generated a mini soap opera in its own right. The means to comprehend Frank's transfiguration into a genuine or at least an honorary Brit lies with the representation of the Bruno family – nuclear and extended.

Laura is white, but Frank does not menace her white femininity; he complements it. Nobody makes cracks about Beauty and the beast when they are around. Laura's declaration of love for the Big Man was the pivot of the TV spectacle. 'Tyson hasn't got what Frank's got,' she intoned, suddenly looking serious, and somehow made the adoration of all Frank's fans an extension of her own personal passion for him. What exactly has Frank got that Tyson lacks? Laura? A British passport? A stable and orthodox domestic set-up?

Contemporary British racism deals in cultural difference rather than crude biological hierarchy. It asserts not that blacks are inferior but that we are different, so different that our distinctive mode of being is at odds with residence in this country. Roughly speaking, black settlers of 'Afro-Caribbean' descent are deemed to be incapable of subscribing to the designated standards of acceptable cultural conduct, whereas comparable 'Asians', even if they possess the potential to meet these standards, lack the requisite inclination. The Goldilocks-and-the-three-bears theory affirms that this too is a matter of simple common sense. The cultural character of this form of racism differentiates it from earlier forms but it is important for at least two other reasons. First, it aligns race and nation very closely together, and second, the family is identified as the primary means through which the inappropriate, deviant and incompatible cultures of resident blacks are illegitimately reproduced to form the oxymoronic 'second-generation immigrant'. 'Afro-Caribbean' families are weak and disorganized, while their 'Asian' equivalents are equally damned for being excessively durable and much too scrupulous in the tasks of cultural transmission.

As the post-war idea of the British Commonwealth as a family of nations began to date and fade, a more sinister vision of the British race as a nation of neatly symmetrical families began to replace it. Against this background, even before they acquired a marriage certificate, Frank's immediate family was cast in the image of the acceptable majority rather than the deviant Caribbean alternative. His partner's whiteness redeemed him from the curse of his ethnicity and provided a means to escape the fortifications of cultural alterity. The fundamental image of domestic harmony which surrounds Frank, Laura and their daughters enables the national community to be presented as an extension of the Bruno clan – one big, happy family. Frank himself compensates for the absence of his own father through the force of his own devotion to that role. We have already met his mother and for most public purposes his manager, Terry Lawless, operates as an authoritative father surrogate. Harry Carpenter made his own bid for the part in a post-fight *Mirror* article where he confided his secret wish that the saintly Frank could have been *his* son. Carpenter would be a prominent figure in media accounts of Bruno's eventual marriage.

The cultural character of today's racism also accentuates ethnic differences *within* the black communities. Some of what were once black communities are now happily shrugging off that label. The precarious political grouping, which for a brief, precious moment during the late 1970s allowed settlers from all the corners of the Empire to find some meaning in an open definition of the term 'black', has been all but destroyed. Today, polite 'anti-racist' orthodoxies demand an alternative formulation – 'black and Asian'. This involves the sacrifice of significant political advantages but is presented as a step forward, a means to remind ourselves that by invoking the term 'black', we are not 'Africanizing' our struggles or declaring everybody to be the same.

Like the activities of his *alter ego*, Lenny Henry, whose own domicile with a white woman was recently attacked by racists, Frank's rise is a significant index of the fragmentation of this older black politics. It is no accident that it was Lenny's appropriation of Frank's linguistic signature 'Know what I mean, Harry?' which triggered the boxer's meteoric ascent into the public eye. Frank, like Lenny's sometime principal character Delbert Wilkins, occasionally threatens to become an embarrassment. But his assertive and provocative occupation of the contested space between blackness and Englishness merits cautious support. The story of his sporting defeat and domestic triumph offers a rich perspective on new patterns of racial realignment. However, the clamour of calls for black and white to unite and fight for the World Heavyweight Championship cannot conceal a new political problem. What do we say when the political and cultural gains of the emergent black Brits go hand in hand with a further marginalization of 'Asians' in general and Muslims in particular?

PART TWO

Diaspora identities, diaspora aesthetics

6 Cruciality and the frog's perspective

An agenda of difficulties for the black arts movement in Britain

Perspectives must be fashioned that displace and estrange the world, reveal it to be, with its rifts and crevices, as indigent and distorted as it will appear one day in the messianic light.

T. W. Adorno

It is of the reactions, tortured and turbulent, of those Asians and Africans, in the New and Old World, that I wish to speak to you. Naturally I cannot speak for those Asians and Africans who are still locked in their mystical or ancestor worshipping traditions. They are the voiceless ones, the silent ones. Indeed, I think that they are the doomed ones, men in a tragic trap. Any attempt on their part to wage battle to protect their traditions and their religions is a battle that is lost before it starts. And I say frankly that I suspect any white man who loves to dote upon these 'naked nobles', who wants to leave them as they are, who finds them 'primitive and pure', for such mystical hankering is, in my opinion, the last refuge of reactionary racists and psychological cripples tired of their own civilisation.

Richard Wright

This paper was read at the conference *Critical Difference: Race, Ethnicity & Culture*, Southampton University, 22 October 1988, organized by John Hansard Gallery as part of the programme during Rasheed Araeen's retrospective, *From Modernism to Postmodernism, 1959–1987.* It was originally published in *Third Text* in 1989.

It has become commonplace to remark that it is in art alone that the consciousness of adversity can find its own voice or consolation without being immediately betrayed by it. In the ironic milieu of racial politics, where the most brutally dispossessed people have often also proved to be the most intensely creative, the idea that artists are representative public figures has become an extra burden for them to carry. Its weight can be felt in the tension between the two quite different senses of a word which refers not just to depiction but to the idea of delegation or substitution.

For black Britain, the supposedly representative practice of avowedly political artists obliges them to speak on behalf of a heterogeneous collectivity.[1] In this case, it is a grouping produced by poverty, racism, exploitation and subordination rather than spontaneous fellow feeling or collective purpose. This community is largely insouciant as far as the problems of the black artist or the black intellectual are concerned. But the ambiguous identity that community provides affords the black artist certain significant protections and compensations. We must begin therefore with the black artist as a public figure – a figure in public politics. The public sphere in which artist and people encounter each other does not coincide neatly with the contours of the British nation-state. The discontinuous histories of black populations in the United States, Africa, Asia, the Caribbean and Europe have contributed to the distinctive experiences of blacks in this country for several hundred years. The communicative networks produced across the Atlantic triangle are *pre*-colonial, and understanding their complex effects is only obscured by simplistic appeals to the unifying potency of an overarching 'colonial discourse'. This point can be extended by saying that, although this paper is primarily concerned with black Britain as a distinct location within the African diaspora, there are other diasporas which contribute directly to the experiences of black

Britain. The traumas of migration, dispersal and exile may themselves have become potent forces in the formation of sororial political relations between groups whose memories of colonial society might otherwise serve only to accentuate the divisions between them. The histories of these different 'racial' groups, though connected, are markedly different even if the effects of racism contain a future promise of their reconciliation.

The value of the term 'diaspora' increases as its essentially symbolic character is understood. It points emphatically to the fact that there can be no pure, uncontaminated or essential blackness anchored in an unsullied originary moment. It suggests that a myth of shared origins is neither a talisman which can suspend political antagonisms nor a deity invoked to cement a pastoral view of black life that can answer the multiple pathologies of contemporary racism.

Artists who would climb out of the underground spaces that serve as the foundations for the British black arts movement, have developed a special skill. They must learn to address different constituencies simultaneously. The most politically astute of them anticipate not a single, uniform audience but a plurality of publics. These audiences often coexist within the same physical environment but they live non-synchronously. Cultural activists encounter them as a hierarchy in which profoundly antagonistic relations may exist between dominant and subordinate groups. Making sense of this configuration of publics and the aura of novelty currently being constructed around black art, requires both artist and critic to consider the difficulties that surround the heretical suggestion that white audiences may be becoming more significant in the development of British black art than any black ones. We must be prepared to assess the differential impact of white audiences on the mood and style of black cultural activism as well as its forms and its ideological coherence.

These questions necessarily assume different proportions in

discussion of vernacular culture than they do in the increasingly rarefied atmosphere that shrouds more self-consciously 'high cultural' black film practice or black visual arts. The question of audience is thus answered differently in each sector of cultural expression. However, the problem of negotiating the relationship between vernacular and non-vernacular forms, like the related problem of admitting to or ignoring white audiences, has become a constant source of uncertainty and friction. It is useful to consider the example of music at this point, not only because it nurtures the 'sui-generis black genius'[2] but because, as the dominant and primary mode of black cultural activism, it supplies a hermeneutic key to a medley of interrelated forms. Articulated in an aesthetic of performance which asserts the priority of expression over artefact, its special traditions of improvisation and antiphony are revealed to be more than merely technical attributes. The deeply encoded language that supports the social relations in which black music is actively consumed has proved to be an additional resource for artists working in a variety of media.

The specifics of black visual arts and film as determinedly non-vernacular forms made by and for the literate and displayed through some of the most marginal distributive networks that England's moribund cultural order can offer, must also be understood. It is a small step on from raising these questions to ask whether these contrasting yet equally black forms demand different political alliances.

Vernacular forms derive their conspicuous power and dynamism in part from the simple fact that they seek to avoid the prying eyes and ears of the white world, whereas black film production in particular is tightly shackled into a relationship of dependency on overground cultural institutions which are both capital- and labour-intensive. When, then, is it becoming illegitimate to ask how different are the black audiences for these forms from the white? This can be a polite way of formulating a deeper and more shocking question: namely, is there *any* black audience for some of the most highly prized products of the black arts movement? Is there a non-literate, black, working- or non-working-class audience eagerly anticipating these particular cultural products? Have 'our' film-makers given up the pursuit of an audience outside the immediate, symbiotic formation in which black 'filmic texts' originate?[3]

Getting a clear picture of these important issues and the questions of class and power that they inescapably entail is actively suppressed by the racial ideology of our times. Contemporary British political orthodoxy around 'race' endorses the idea that racial identities are somehow primary, yet their supposed importance is matched by fear of their increasing fragility. It is sometimes argued that these identities are so frail that they are threatened by the fact that black and white people may want to discuss questions of aesthetics and politics together. Meanwhile, the complex pluralism of Britain's inner-urban streets demonstrates that, among the poor, elaborate syncretic processes are under way. This is not simple integration, but a complex, non-linear phenomenon. Each contributory element is itself transformed in their coming together. The kaleidoscopic formations of 'trans-racial' cultural syncretism are growing daily more detailed and more beautiful. Yet where black art and aesthetics are debated in conference after conference it is becoming harder to dislodge the belief that ethnic differences constitute an absolute break in history and humanity. A commitment to the mystique of cultural insiderism and the myths of cultural homogeneity is alive not just among the Brit-nationalists and racists but among the anti-racists who strive to answer them. The rampant popularity of these opinions dissolves old ideas of left and right and is directly connected to a dangerous variety of political timidity that culminates in a reluctance to debate some racial subjects because they are too sensitive to be aired and too volatile to be discussed openly. A corresponding tide of anti-intellectualism has meant that some spokespeople inside the black communities have accepted the trap which racism lays and begun to celebrate an idea of themselves as people who are happy to feel rather than think. It is also significant that this strong attachment to ethnicity has appeared as class relations inside the black communities are in turmoil. We must face the fact that our communities are increasingly riven by class antagonism. Certain cultural forms, for example the travel writing of Salman Rushdie and Caryl Phillips, clearly aspire to be part of the making of the black middle class.

This peculiar situation demands that we return to some old issues: the autonomy of art and the issue of racial propaganda; whether the protest and affirmation couplet is an adequate framework for understanding black cultural politics. In what sense are artists to be loyal only to themselves? Can the obligations of black consciousness and artistic freedom be complementary rather than mutually exclusive? Can there be a revolutionary core to what Richard Wright once called the aesthetics of 'personalism' and the matching politics of radical individualism which have characterized Western modernisms – their academicism, formal preoccupations and imaginative proximity to social revolution? Nowadays, these historic questions tend to appear in somewhat different form and in a wholly different conceptual vocabulary. They are present in the suggestion that something called 'post-modernism' may provide a ready-made 'decentering of imperial and patriarchal discourses'. They haunt Michael Thelwell's repeated suggestion that modernism for black artists is an indulgence or evasion of their unique responsibilities, and Houston Baker's provocative but rather sketchy remarks on the ways in which the idea of modernism might be rethought as part of the intellectual and political history of Afro-America.[4]

A preliminary resolution of these problems may lie in embracing an aesthetic and political strategy that many black artists have evolved in an apparently spontaneous manner. I will call this option 'populist modernism',[5] a deliberately contradictory term which suggests that black artists are not only both 'defenders and critics of modernism' but mindful of their historic obligation to interrogate the dubious legacies of occidental modernity premised on the exclusion of blacks. This distinctive aesthetic and ethico-political approach requires a special gloss on terms like reason, justice, freedom and 'communicative ethics'. It starts from recognition of the African diaspora's peculiar position as 'step-children' of the West and of the extent to which our imaginations are conditioned by an enduring proximity to regimes of racial terror. It seeks deliberately to exploit the distinctive quality of perception that Du Bois identified long ago as 'double conciousness'.[6] Whether this is viewed as an effect of oppression or a unique moral burden, it is premised on some sense of black cultures, not simply as significant repositories of anti-capitalist sensibility but as counter-cultures of modernity forged in the quintessentially modern condition of racial slavery.

The most basic formal expression of this approach is recognizable in the recurrent desire of black artists to re-articulate the positive core of aesthetic modernism into resolutely populist formats. The fiction of Richard Wright, Toni Morrison, Alice Walker and Cyrus Coulter, James Brown's music, Amiri Baraka's drama and criticism, and even Lenny Henry's recent performances in the role of Delbert Wilkins, provide myriad examples. However, 'populist modernism' does not simply mark out adventuresome black borrowings and adaptations from a pre-formed Western canon. It can also apply where autonomous and self-validating non-European expressive traditions have entered the institutionalized Western world of art and, most importantly, where the historical and cultural substance of black life in the

West has spontaneously arrived at insights which appear in European traditions as the exclusive results of lengthy and lofty philosophical speculation. For example, some of the prized linguistic insights of post-structuralism are less than novel in the context of a cultural tradition in which writing, liberation and auto-poesis are inextricably entangled. In an interesting polemic against the idea of 'black studies' C. L. R. James illuminates this point by describing an encounter with Richard Wright.[7]

Having gone to the country to spend the weekend with Wright and his family, James describes being ushered into their house and shown numerous volumes of Kierkegaard, Heidegger, Nietzsche and Husserl on the bookshelves. Wright, fresh from cooking chicken in the kitchen, points to the bound volumes, saying 'Look here Nello, you see those books there? . . . Everything that [they] write in those books I knew before I had them.' James suggests that Wright's apparently intuitive foreknowledge of the issues raised by Kierkegaard and the rest was an elementary product of his historical experiences as a black growing up in the United States between the wars: 'What [Dick] was telling me was that he was a black man in the United States and that gave him an insight into what today is the universal opinion and attitude of the *modern* personality' (my emphasis).

This historic meeting of two great black minds constitutes an important cautionary tale for Britain's black arts movement. For one thing, it supplies a timely reminder that art history and criticism do not supply adequate answers to their own parochial questions. If we also remember that non-European expressive traditions have refused the caesura which Western high culture would introduce between art and life, the insights of Wright and James can also be read as an implicit questioning of the idea that occidental aesthetics and philosophy are best understood as cohesive yet autonomous projects. It is also a great relief to discover that these issues have been dealt with before by the artists and thinkers of the African diaspora. Yet their tradition of inquiry into what can loosely be called the politics of representation is itself obscure. It needs to be recovered and brought into debates which are just beginning in black Britain. Certain aspects of the aesthetic and philosophical traditions of the diaspora are particularly pertinent to black Britain's conditions of exile, voluntary and involuntary. First, an understanding of 'racial' memory in affective and normative terms rather than as a problem of cognition is particularly pressing. Second, much work needs to be done on the distinctive intertextual patterns in which discrete texts and performances have echoed each other, corresponded, interacted and replied. Third, forms of black meta-communication, which require that surface and deep expressions diverge, pose special analytical problems. Fourth, the centrality of performance rather than text and the consequent priority accorded to the act of expression over the artefact require a distinct methodological orientation. These modes of signification render the arbitrary relation between signs and referents in its most radical form. It cannot be said too often that they originate in a historical experience where the error of mistaking a sign for its referent becomes quite literally a matter of life and death. Fifth, these traditions have had plenty to say about the polysemic richness of black languages that pose a question mark over the adequacy of language in general as a vehicle for articulating the intensity of meaning that diaspora history necessitates. Finally, there is the problem of genre and the constant subversive desire originally clearly evident in the auto-poesis of the slave autobiography to blend and transcend key Western categories: narrative and documentary; history and literature; ethics and politics; word and sound. Why, for example, was it necessary for Du Bois's *The Souls of Black Folk* to bring together sociology, history, music and fiction into a unified, polyphonic cultural performance?

This new agenda means that it is no longer enough simply to recognize the dialogic features of these forms before comparing their supposed openness to the closed monologues of the master discourses of the master race. The specific forms which that dialogism takes must themselves be probed. A gospel choir and soloist, an improvising jazz band, a reggae toaster, a scratch mixer and Keith Piper have all developed the dialogic character of black expressive culture in different directions. Their expressive forms are dialogic, but that dialogism is of a special type and its irreducible complexity has moved beyond the grasp of the self/other dichotomy.

Identifying what these different performances might share and making explicit the deep and carefully concealed aesthetic and political structures that make sense of them requires additional, supplementary concepts. All, for example, play with the principle of antiphony (call and response), a term which is particularly appropriate because it underlies the special role of black musics in articulating non-verbal – unspoken and unspeakable – formulations of ethics and aesthetics. Approaching contemporary black cultural politics by this route involves a sharp move away from the rigid nexus of modernism and post-modernism and the casual references to the 'technical successes of modernist culture' which emanate from it. It is a tenacious challenge to the nascent orthodoxies of post-modernism which can only see the distinctive formal features of black expressive culture in terms of pastiche, quotation, parody and paraphrase rather than a more substantive, political and aesthetic concern with polyphony and the value of different registers of address.

This leads directly to the significance of current debates around post-modernism for the British black arts movement. There are special reasons why black activists here should resist the idea that any struggle over images is necessarily a struggle over power. The problems in trying to hold the term together are now well known: how does it refer to modernization, what are its claims as a cognitive theory, is it doing more than merely register a change in the cultural climate? Can the logic of late capitalism be marked conceptually in a non-reductive way? I see no strong objection to the term as a purely heuristic device. But there is a tendency to make it something more than this, to use it as the conceptual cornerstone of another grand narrative – several perhaps – as well as fuel for the resolutely uncritical academic industry currently being built in Britain around the excuses it offers – what Zygmunt Bauman has called its philosophy of surrender.[8] Post-modernism fever is an ailment identified through symptoms that have been around within modernism for a long while. François Lyotard's ties to C. L. R. James through the Socialisme ou Barbarie group, and Fredric Jameson's appetite for a rather anachronistic 'base and superstructure' variety of Marxism, betoken some of the more significant continuities. These ties may be an indication that the grand narrative of reason is not currently being brought to an end but rather *transformed*. Forms of rationality are being created endlessly. Perhaps only European hubris claims that this particular moment of crisis is the fundamental moment of rupture, the new dawn. Another significant way in which post-modernist orthodoxy is reconstitutive of earlier, more obviously modernist, work is its persistence in dealing with the problem of the subject exclusively in terms of its formation rather than through the fundamental issues of agency, action, reason and rationality inherent in considering the relationship between master and slave. Robert Farris Thompson's provocative discussion of Ashe, the ancient Yoruba concept of the power to make things happen, shows that these do not have to be Eurocentric issues.[9] The strategic silences in post-modernist pronouncements constitute a glimpse of the sad predicament of a coterie of ailing Western intellectuals comforting themselves on the historic funeral pyre of their class with a hot water-bottle of realism. This gesture abdicates their responsibility, not to some abstract 'other' but to themselves. To point this out is not to say that I think older, grander formulations have any residual appeal. The only happy moment in this whole unsavoury explosion of enthusiasm for the 'post-modern' is its challenge to the theological authority of positivistic Marxism. We should not have to choose between the knackered phallocracy of the vanguard party and an 'anything goes' or 'anything does' position which, at its best, simply places a pluralist or 'realist' mask in front of genuine conservatism. At its worst, post-modernism fever offers an exclusively aesthetic radicalism as the substitute for a moral one.

> . . . the new political art if it is to be possible at all – will have to hold to the truth of post-modernism, that is to say, to its fundamental object – the world space of multi-national capital – at the same time at which it achieves a breakthrough to some as yet unimaginable new mode of representing this last, in which we may again begin to grasp our positioning as individual and collective subjects and regain a capacity to act and struggle which is at present neutralised by our spatial as well as our social confusion.[10]

It is time that Professor Jameson specified precisely who is included when he says 'we' and 'our'. Those of us who have been denied access to the diachronic payoff that people like him take for granted are just beginning to formulate our own grand narratives. They are narratives of redemption and emancipation. Our cultural politics is not therefore about depthlessness but about depth, not about the waning of affect but about its reproduction, not about the suppression of temporal patterns but about history itself. This realization is our cue to shift the centre of debate away from Europe, to look at other more peripheral encounters with modernity. It is worth underlining that for some of us the 'enthusiasm of 1789' relates more to Port au Prince than it does to Paris. Why is it so difficult to think through the relationship between these locations and their respective counter-powers? To put it another way, it is not just the 'annihilation named Auschwitz' which now requires a formal transformation of what counts as history and as reality, of our understanding of reference and the function of the proper name. These ethico-political problems have been the substance of black expressive culture since slavery; from the time we walked through the door of Christianity and became people of the West (in it but not organically of it) and acquired the 'double vision' that entails what Richard Wright, drawing on Nietzsche, called the Frog's Perspective.[11]

Wright is one of the handful of black writers who have seen black nationalism as a beginning rather than an end. His populist modernism, most cogently expressed in his 1953 novel *The Outsider*, is crucial not least because it allows for the possibility that non-black artists may be part of the inheritance of black artists. This is only one way of rethinking the question of racial identity, secure in the knowledge that people inhabit highly differentiated and complex, even de-centred, identities. Race carries with it no fixed corona of absolute meanings. Thus gender, class, culture and even locality may become more significant determinants of identity than either biological phenotype or the supposed cultural essences of what are now known as ethnic groups. Culture is not a final property of social life. It is a dynamic volatile force. It is made and remade and the culture of the English fragments of the black diaspora is a syncretic, synthetic one. This ought to be obvious but it is not. The most unwholesome ideas of ethnic absolutism hold sway and they have been incorporated into the structures of the political economy of funding black arts. The tokenism, patronage and nepotism that have become intrinsic to the commodification of black culture rely absolutely on an absolute sense of ethnic difference. This variety of absolutism is strongest and most theoretically coherent in non-vernacular cultural forms. It is most eloquent where white audiences are not simply assumed but actively sought out and where the glamour of ambivalent ethnicity borrows most heavily from the devious, rhetorical excesses of literary post-structuralism.

Happily, there are elements within Britain's emergent post-nationalist black arts movement that are prepared to move as earlier generations of black intellectuals and artists have done, not into the blind alley of ethnic particularity, but outwards into a global, populist-modernist perspective.

At this point, the word 'sponditious', Delbert Wilkins's favourite term of praise, provides an appropriate conceptual marker for a new relationship, between the black artist and the racial community. Misrecognized by the overground as nonsense rather than good sense, it asserts the primacy of the vernacular over the esoteric and specifies the redemptive uniqueness of emergent black-English cultural forms. Sponditiousness is a vital presence in the antiphonic work of a host of little-known photographers, film-makers and writers.

However difficult their work becomes, it is always aligned to vernacular forms and modes of expression. The underground is the source of their joyously productive break with the immediate political past and their striking ability to perceive 'race' not as a biological or even cultural essence but as an inherently unstable social and political construction. There is also a hesitant, tentative suggestion that the most urgent tasks of black artists might begin in the critical documentation and dismantling of those constructed differences, not just between black and white but within the black communities too. These cultural activists do not articulate blackness as a homogenous condition. Their work testifies to the fact that it is riven by gender, sexuality, generation and class. Their primary difficulty is that if they know where black art is to begin, they do not necessarily understand where it is to end: in what has been called the black artist's search for space and status? Space where? Status with whom? In the transcendence of 'racial' particularity? In defensive political action? At present, there is every danger that these questions will be buried by an enthusiasm for the dubious comforts provided by the belief in an eternal ethnic identity and a theory of postmodernism that is little more than a premature foreclosure of vital debate. Pre-emptive statements that invoke the authority of the very grand narratives they are supposedly committed to deconstructing suggest, for example, that an integration of Afro-Asian cultures in contemporary Britain is simply nostalgic.[12] But why should this be the case? If we accept the necessarily pluralistic and polyphonic character of black culture, if we understand syncretism as the organizing and disorganizing principle at work in the cultural lives of black city-dwellers who may never have lived anywhere else, then the forms of this supposedly naive desire to integrate may already be spontaneously under way.

The critical tools which will unlock and discipline this new movement of black arts are at present in an undeveloped foetal state. The movement's inspiration lies in an exploration of the idea of blackness in relation to the idea of Britishness, but this project does not even attempt to explain how blackness is itself to be understood. If it is not a primary identity, is it a metaphysical condition? Can it be a bit of both? Was Ellison right when he suggested that it is a state of the soul accessible to all? Or was Baldwin correct when he articulated it as a mark of pain and hardship which carries with it a special obligation to humanize the dry bones of modernity's arid landscapes? How are we to think of difference within the framework it provides? Can we, like the D-Max group of photographers[13] did with the clever name for their collective, find symbols to express a multiplicity of black tones? Perhaps the realization that blackness is a necessarily multi-accentual sign provides a means to escape either/or-ism. Blackness evolves in fractal patterns. What we can usefully say about it depends on the scale of the analysis which is being undertaken. It is only when viewed from above that Britain's black communities have the homogeneity of a neat Euclidean outline. Moving lower and closer reveals the infinite course of their expressive traditions even within a highly restricted space – the fractal geometry of black life's rifts and crevices. Expressive culture can, of course, provide a means for different groups to negotiate each other's definitions of what it means to be black in overdeveloped, besieged Britain now. There are several other things we need to be clear on before we proceed. It may be easier to talk about racism than about black emancipation but there is inevitably more to black art and life than any answers they give to racism.

If our artists are to be primarily judged on the basis of their answers to racism, and that is a real danger at present, it must also be borne in mind that racism changes. There is, for example, no point in answering culturalist racism with artistic and political tactics appropriate to biological definitions of race. We must also recognize how racism pushes those it subordinates outside history into the unacceptable twin forms of the problem and the victim. These repellent roles exist only in an unchanging present. A reply to this effect of racist discourse and practice can only be produced by representing black life in terms of active agency, however limited its scope. Problems over the relation of aesthetics, ethics and politics are further compounded by the question of how a sense of historical process, generational continuity and change can be restored. Here, we can begin to engage with the specific history of blacks in Britain and this is a far more complex matter than it appears from the preliminary pioneering

work which has already been done. None of us enjoys a monopoly on black authenticity.

The inescapable tension between those who define themselves
as artists or intellectuals and the mass of the black settler communities cannot be conjured away. I am suggesting that only by
sharpening that antagonism can we make our notion of community a way of having disagreements productively among ourselves rather than a largely rhetorical means of rationalizing the
domination and subordination which already exists.

Notes

Thanks to Vron Ware, Karen Alexander, Isaac Julien, David A. Bailey, Kobena
Mercer and Sonia Boyce who helped me put this together. We're droppin'
science y'all.

1. A useful starting point for enquiries into the inner character of the black
arts movement in Britain is provided by *Storm of the Heart*, edited by Kwesi
Owusu, Camden Press, London 1988. Catalogues produced for black art
exhibitions: *The Thin Black Line*, Institute of Contemporary Art, London,
1985; *The Essential Black Art*, Chisenhale Gallery, London, 1988; *The Image
Employed: The Use of Narrative in Black Art*, Cornerhouse, Manchester,
1987; *From Modernism to Postmodernism: Rashed Araeen/A Retrospective
1959–1987*, Ikon Gallery, Birmingham, 1987–88; *From Two Worlds*,
Whitechapel Gallery, London, 1986; *Sonia Boyce*, Air Gallery, London, 1986;
Black British Film Culture, ICA Document No. 7, ICA, London.
2. Greg Tate, 'The Return of the Black Aesthetic Cult. Nats meet Freaky-
Deke', *Village Voice* Literary Supplement, December 1986; 'Public Enemy, The
Devil Made 'Em Do It', *Village Voice*, 19 July 1988; 'Uplift the Race', *Village
Voice*, 22 March 1988.
3. This point came home to me forcefully when I received a press release
from the Black Audio Film Collective, prize-winning authors of the celebrated
Handsworth Songs. This press release chronicled the success of *Handsworth
Songs* and its successor, their latest film, *Testament*:

> *Testament*, Black Audio Film Collective's new film, has won the
> 1988 Grand Prize at the Riminincinema International Film Festival

in Italy. The award follows *Testament*'s premiere at the Cannes
International Film Festival (May) and its subsequent screenings at
the Munich Film Festival (June), Montreal World Film Festival
(August), Toronto Festival of Festivals (September) and its British
premiere at the Birmingham International Film Festival (September).

It is possible that the group had simply overlooked or forgotten the possibility
that black British film culture might have a different agenda of priorities from
that set by international film festival circuits. On the other hand, they may be
simply making explicit what we had all suspected, namely that there is no base
or context for the type of films they want to make within the black
communities in this country.

   4. Michael Thelwell, *Duties, Pleasures and Conflicts*, University of
Massachusetts Press, 1987; Houston Baker, *Modernism and the Harlem
Renaissance*, Chicago University Press, 1987.
   5. I borrowed this term from Werner Sollor's study *Amiri Baraka/Leroi
Jones: The Quest for a Populist Modernism*, Columbia University Press, 1978.
   6. See W. E. B. Du Bois, *The Souls of Black Folk*, Bantam, New York, 1989
and Robert C. Williams's 'W. E. B. Du Bois: Afro-American philosopher of
social reality' in L. Harris (ed.), *Philosophy Born of Struggle*, Kendall Hunt,
Iowa, 1983.
   7. C. L. R. James, 'Black Studies and the Contemporary Student' in *At The
Rendez-vous with Victory*, Allison & Busby, London, 1984.
   8. Zygmunt Bauman, 'The Left as the Counterculture of Modernity', *Telos
70*, 1986–87.
   9. Robert Farris Thompson, *Flash of the Spirit: African and Afro-American
Art and Philosophy*, Vintage Books, New York, 1983.
   10. Fredric Jameson, 'Postmodernism or the Cultural Logic of Late
Capitalism', *NLR 146*, July/August 1984.
   11. Richard Wright, 'Preface' to George Padmore's *Pan Africanism or
Communism*, Dennis Dobson, London, 1956.
   12. John Roberts, 'Postmodernism and the Critique of Ethnicity: The recent
work of Rasheed Araeen' in the catalogue *From Modernism to
Postmodernism*, Ikon Gallery, Birmingham, 1987.
   13. *D-Max* catalogue, Photographers Gallery, London, 1988.

7   D-Max

Long ago, in his 'Blueprint'* for black artists, Richard Wright asserted the necessity of collective work in the development of black expression. Wright saw this mode of working as an indispensable strategy in circumstances where the fragmentation of the African diaspora and the systemic turbulence of the modern world – its economic and political crises – meant that for black artists 'tradition is no longer a guide'.

Although it emerges from a different period and from different strands of black history, the D-Max exhibition represents the fulfilment of a similar commitment. The six photographers whose work is on display have been meeting together to discuss and develop their art for over two years. Their contrasting styles and approaches have been refined and strengthened in a process of mutual criticism and collective support which has become essential to the realization of individual concerns. Their collaboration is thus more than a joint assault on the mainstream institutions of the art world which marginalize and trivialize black expression by relegating it to the necessary but insufficient role of documentary.

This chapter is the text of the 1988 catalogue from the D-Max exhibition.

*'Blueprint for Negro Writing', *New Challenge*, Fall 1937, reprinted *Race and Class*, 21, 4, Spring 1980, pp. 403–12.

Work by Ingrid, D-Max

The unity within diversity which is an explicit feature of this exhibition betrays deeper political concerns. It can be read as a bold and significant intervention in recent debates, not simply about black aesthetics but about the meaning and status of blackness itself in contemporary Britain. The choice of 'D-Max' as a name for the group alludes not simply to a technical command of their chosen medium of expression, but to the range of blacks that a photographic emulsion can offer. It is a neat symbol of the photographers' awareness of the aesthetic and political plurality of blackness – its shades, nuances and uneven contours, its inner contradictions and internal fractures. Blackness is riven by class, gender and generation. It is to be explored as a social and political construction rather than simply accepted as an unchanging essence or a cultural absolute. Like racism itself, it is understood as a changing same. This insight suggests that a black aesthetic can only emerge after a careful examination of precisely what it means to be black here and now. This in turn requires focusing on the aesthetic and political framework of the diaspora and the cultural exchanges or conversations which those frameworks facilitate between Britain's black settlers and black populations elsewhere. Marc Boothe's extended exploration of black musicians in performance is thus more than an important enquiry into the relationship between black photographic practice and other more obviously vernacular forms of black cultural expression. These pictures constitute a celebratory acknowledgement of the contribution which the musical traditions of Afro-America have made to contemporary black sensibility in this country. The enduring impact of this musical tradition is one crucial factor in determining what it means to be black in Britain today.

Music provides only the most obvious example of how the specific, local and immediate meanings of blackness are actively produced rather than passively inherited. Contemporary black culture in Britain is not a finished artefact waiting to be simply unlocked from inside the earlier and rather different experiences of 'racial' kin in Africa, America and the Caribbean. It is a unique process, nurtured where discontinuous histories of powerlessness and empire have fed into distinctively English experiences to produce new patterns of struggle, negotiation and intimacy. Giving priority to the immediate and local content of black experience is not a betrayal of its other dimensions but rather a tacit acknowledgement that the form of racial politics constantly changes. D Max is inviting the viewer to see the effects of these local 'black English' experiences in their wider cultural and political context. This is supplied by valuable and powerful 'raw material' produced by non-European populations elsewhere. You are being asked to consider where these different histories combine and mediate each other and how blackness is produced by their association.

The specific construction of racial difference and identity in contemporary Britain emerges as a central theme around which several of the contributors have structured their own improvisations. It acquires a particular power in Ingrid Pollard's Lake District sequence and David A. Bailey's shots of the British Museum's Egyptian holdings. In developing this argument, several of the pieces directly confront Britishness and Englishness, two key categories in today's cultural racism. This concern is a way of attacking the manner in which that racism has sought to make Englishness and blackness mutually exlusive – a problem which is explicitly addressed in Dave Lewis's carefully constructed work. However, the exhibition's public negotiation of Britain and Englishness is part of a wider examination of ambiguity and belonging that culminates in a more general argument about the highly differentiated and complex nature of individual identity.

Above all, the collective character of this exhibition and the pluralistic sense artist or group can claim a monopoly of authentic 'racial' expression. The group's deliberately and provocatively polyphonic approach is further underscored by the range of different techniques they have employed. Gilbert John's skilful use of colour contributes as vigorously to their aesthetic as the more obviously combative black-and-white material. The use of text alongside images suggests that the sheer intensity of 'racial' feeling requires more than either words or pictures can offer on their own.

The group's thoroughly unfashionable way of understanding the development of black art and politics in Britain articulates a challenge to the facile orthɔdoxies on black art and culture that are increasingly shared by voices both inside and outside the black community. These views can be defined, first by their sense of blackness as a homogenous and simple category and second, by their belief that black art must be understood primarily as a reaction – a response to racism. Whatever its sources, this drive towards simplicity can also be identified by the disproportionate emphasis it places on simplistic cultural definitions of 'race'. Black culture is seen as a closed legacy which fixes all the coordinates of contemporary black life. If black artists are to be successful, they must learn to be content either with reworking supposedly traditional concerns or with documenting the undeniable suffering of the black communities.

D-Max breaks implicitly with these beliefs in affirming that there is more to black art and expressive culture than the answers they supply to racial subordination. This exhibition points to the irreducible complexity of black life and then defends the idea that artists must be loyal principally to themselves. Its historic importance in the development of black arts in Britain is to show that the precious autonomy of the black artist need not be bought at the price of disengagement from wider ethical and political concerns.

8 It ain't where you're from, it's where you're at

The dialectics of diaspora identification

Music is our witness, and our ally. The beat is the confession which recognizes, changes and conquers time. Then, history becomes a garment we can wear and share, and not a cloak in which to hide; and time becomes a friend.

James Baldwin

No nation now but the imagination.

Derek Walcott

The subject of this paper is culture and resistance and I want to begin by asking you to consider how resistance itself is to be understood. I think that our recent political history, as people in but not necessarily of the modern, Western world, a history which involves processes of political organization that are explicitly transcultural and international in nature, demands that we consider this question very carefully. What is being resisted and by what means? Slavery? Capitalism? Coerced industrialization? Racial terror? Or ethnocentrism and European solipsism? How are the discontinuous, plural histories of diaspora resistance to be *thought*, to be theorized by those who have experienced the consequences of racial domination?

This chapter was originally published in *Third Text* in 1991.

In this paper, I want to look specifically at the positions of the nation-state, and the idea of nationality in accounts of black resistance and black culture, particularly music. Towards the end, I will also use a brief discussion of black music to ask implicit questions about the tendencies towards ethnocentrism and ethnic absolutism of black cultural theory. The problem of weighing the claims of national identity against other contrasting varieties of subjectivity and identification has a special place in the intellectual history of blacks in the West. W. E. B. Du Bois's concept of 'double consciousness'[1] is only the best-known resolution of a familiar problem which points towards the core dynamic of racial oppression as well as the fundamental antinomy of diaspora blacks. How has this doubleness, what Richard Wright calls the 'dreadful objectivity'[2] which flows from being both inside and outside the West, affected the conduct of political movements against racial oppression and towards black autonomy? Can the inescapable pluralities involved in the movements of black peoples, in Africa and in exile, ever be synchronized? How would these struggles be periodized in relation to modernity: the fatal intermediation of capitalism, industrialization and a new conception of political democracy? Does even posing these questions in this way signify nothing except the reluctant intellectual affiliation of diaspora blacks to an approach which attempts a premature totalization of our infinite struggles, an approach which has deep roots within the ambiguous intellectual traditions of the European enlightenment?

In my view, the problematic intellectual heritage of Euro-American modernity still determines the manner in which nationality is understood within black political discourse. In particular, it conditions the continuing aspiration to acquire a supposedly authentic, natural and stable identity. This identity is the premise of a thinking 'racial' self that is both socialized and unified by its connection with other kindred souls encountered usually, though not always, within the fortified frontiers of those discrete ethnic cultures which also happen to coincide with the contours of a sovereign nation-state that guarantees their continuity. Consider for a moment the looseness with which the term 'black nationalism' is used both by its advocates and by sceptics. Why is a more refined political language for dealing with these crucial issues of identity, kinship and affiliation such a long time coming?

This area of difficulty has recently become associated with a second, namely the over-integrated conceptions of culture which mean that black political struggles are construed as somehow automatically *expressive* of the national or ethnic differences with which they are articulated. This over-integrated sense of cultural and ethnic particularity is very popular today and blacks do not monopolize it. It masks the arbitrariness of its own political choices in the morally charged language of ethnic absolutism and this poses significant dangers because it overlooks the development of political ideology and ignores the restless, recombinant qualities of our affirmative political cultures. The critical political project forged in the journey from slave ship to citizenship is in danger of being wrecked by the seemingly insoluble conflict between two distinct but currently symbiotic perspectives which can be loosely identified as the essentialist and the pluralist standpoints.

The antagonistic relationship between these outlooks is especially intense in discussions of black art and cultural criticism. The essentialist view comes in gender-specific forms, but has often been characterized by an archaic pan-Africanism that, in Britain at least, is now politically inert. In the newer garb of Africentricity it has still proved unable to specify precisely where the highly prized but doggedly evasive essence of black artistic sensibility is currently located. This perspective sees the black artist as a potential leader. It is often allied to a realist approach to aesthetics which minimizes the substantive political and philosophical issues involved in the processes of artistic representation. Its absolutist conception of ethnic cultures can be identified by the way in which it registers uncomprehending disappointment with the actual cultural choices and patterns of the mass of black people in this country. It looks for an artistic practice that can disabuse them of the illusions into which they have been seduced by their condition of exile. The community is felt to be on the wrong road and it is the artist's job to give them a new direction, first by recovering and then by donating the racial awareness that the masses seem to lack.

This perspective currently confronts a pluralistic position which affirms blackness as an open signifier and seeks to celebrate complex representations of a black particularity that is *internally* divided: by class, sexuality, gender, age and political consciousness. There is no unitary idea of black community here and the authoritarian tendencies of those who would 'police' black cultural expression in the name of their own particular history or priorities are rightly repudiated. Essentialism is replaced by a libertarian alternative: the saturnalia which attends 'the dissolution of the essential black subject'. Here, the polyphonic qualities of black cultural expression form the main aesthetic consideration and there is often an uneasy but exhilarating fusion of 'modernist' and populist techniques and styles. From this perspective, the cultural achievements of popular black cultural forms like music are a constant source of inspiration and are prized for their implicit warning against the pitfalls of artistic conceit. The difficulty with this second tendency is that, in leaving racial essentialism behind by viewing 'race' itself as a social and cultural construction, it has been insufficiently alive to the lingering power of specifically 'racial' forms of power and subordination. Each outlook attempts to compensate for the obvious weaknesses in the other camp but so far there has been little open and explicit debate between them.

This conflict, initially formulated in debates over black aesthetics and cultural production, is valuable as a preliminary guide to some of the dilemmas faced by cultural and intellectual *historians* of the African diaspora. The problems it raises become acute, particularly for those who seek to comprehend cultural developments and political resistances which have had scant regard for either modern borders or pre-modern frontiers. At its worst, the lazy, casual invocation of cultural insiderism which characterizes the essentialist view is nothing more than a melancholy symptom of the growing cleavages *within* the black communities. There, uneasy spokespeople of the black middle classes – some of them professional cultural commentators, artists, writers, painters and film-makers as well as career politicians – have fabricated a volkish political outlook as an expression of their own contradictory position. Although the 'neo' is never satisfactorily explained, this is often presented as a neo-nationalism. It incorporates meditation on the special needs and desires of the relatively privileged castes within black communities, but its most consistent trademark is the persistent mystification of that group's increasingly problematic relationships with the black poor who, after all, supply them with a dubious entitlement to speak on behalf of black people in general.

The idea of blacks as a 'national' or proto-national group with its own hermetically enclosed culture plays a key role in this mystification and, though seldom overtly named, the misplaced idea of a 'national interest' gets invoked here as a means to silence dissent and censor political debate.

These problems take on a specific aspect in Britain, which still lacks anything that can credibly be called a black bourgeoisie. However, they are not confined to this country and they cannot be overlooked. The idea of nationality and the assumptions of cultural absolutism come together in various other ways.[3] For example, the archaeology of black critical knowledges in which we are engaged, currently involves the construction of canons which seems to be proceeding on an exclusively *national* basis – Afro-American, Anglophone Caribbean and so on. (This is not just my oblique answer to the pressure to produce an equivalent inventory of black English or British cultural forms and expressions.) If it seems indelicate to ask whom the formation of such canons might serve, then the related question of where the impulse to formalize and codify elements of our cultural heritage in this particular pattern comes from may be a better one with which to commence.

The historiography of canon formation raises interesting issues for the intellectual historian in and of itself. But if the way that these issues occur around the question of the canon appears too obscure, similar problems are also evident in recent debates over hip-hop culture, the powerful expressive medium of America's urban black poor. Rap is a hybrid form rooted in the syncretic social relations of the South Bronx where Jamaican sound-system culture, transplanted during the 1970s, put down new roots and in conjunction with specific technological innovations, set in train a process that was to transform black America's sense of itself and a large portion of the popular music industry as well. How does a form which flaunts and glories in its own malleability as well as its transnational character become interpreted as an expression of some authentic Afro-American essence? Why is rap discussed as if it sprang intact from the entrails of the blues?[4] What is it about Afro-America's writing elite which means that they need to claim this diasporic cultural form in such an assertively nationalist way?[5] Hip-hop culture has recently provided the raw material for a bitter contest between black vernacular expression and repressive censorship of artistic work. This has thrown some black commentators into a quandary which they resolve by invoking the rhetoric of cultural insiderism and drawing the distinctive cloak of ethnicity even more tightly around their shoulders. It is striking, for example, that apologists for the woman-hating antics of the 2 Live Crew have been so far unconcerned that the vernacular tradition they desire to affirm has its own record of reflection on the specific ethical obligations and political responsibilities which constitute the unique burden of the black artist. This may have generational, even authoritarian, implications because the 'racial' community is always a source of constraint as well as a source of support and protection for its artists and intellectuals but, leaving the question of misogyny aside for a moment, to collude in the belief that black vernacular is *nothing* more than a playfully parodic cavalcade of Rabelaisian subversion decisively weakens the positions of the artist, the critical commentator[6] and the community as a whole. What is more significant is surely the failure of either academic or journalistic commentary on black popular music in America to develop a reflexive political aesthetics capable of distinguishing the 2 Live Crew and their ilk from their equally 'authentic' but possibly more compelling and certainly more constructive peers.[7] I am not suggesting that the self-conscious racial pedagogy of artists like KRS1, The Poor Righteous Teachers, Lakim Shabazz or The X Clan can be straightforwardly counterposed against the carefully calculated affirmative nihilism of Ice Cube, Above The Law and Compton's Most Wanted. The different styles and political perspectives expressed within the music are linked both by the bonds of a stylized but aggressively masculinist discourse and by formal borrowings from the linguistic innovations of Jamaica's distinct traditions of 'kinetic orality'[8]. The debt to Caribbean forms is more openly acknowledged in the ludic Afrocentrisms of The Jungle Brothers, De La Soul and A Tribe Called Quest, which may represent a third alternative – in its respectful and egalitarian representation of women and in its ambivalent relationship to America. This stimulating and innovative work operates a rather different conception of black authenticity which effectively contrasts the local (black nationalism) with the global (black internationalism) and Americanism with Ethiopianism. It is important to emphasize that all three strands within hip-hop contribute to a folk-cultural constellation where neither the political compass of weary leftism nor the shiny navigational instruments of premature black post-modernism[9] in aesthetics offer very much that is useful.

An additional, and possibly more profound, area of political difficulty comes into view where the voguish language of absolute cultural difference I have described provides an embarrassing link between the practice of blacks who comprehend racial politics through it and the activities of their foresworn opponents – the racist New Right – who approach the complex dynamics of race, nationality and ethnicity through a similar set of precise, culturalist equations.

This unlikely convergence must also be analysed. It too leads rapidly and directly back to the status of nationality and national cultures in a post-modern world where nation-states are being eclipsed by a new economy of power which accords national citizenship a new significance. In seeking to account for it we have to explore how the over-integrated, absolutist and exclusivist approach to the relationship between 'race', ethnicity and culture places those who claim to be able to resolve the relationship between incommensurable discourses in command of the cultural resources of the group as a whole. They claim this vanguard position by virtue of an ability to translate from one culture to another, mediating decisive class oppositions along the way. At this point it matters little whether the black communities are conceived as entire and self-sustaining nations or proto-national collectivities. Black intellectuals have persistently succumbed to the lure of those romantic conceptions of 'race', 'people' and 'nation' which place themselves, rather than the people they supposedly represent, in charge of the strategies for nation-building, state formation and racial uplift.

This point again underscores the fact that the status of nationality and the precise weight we should attach to the conspicuous differences of language, culture and identity which divide the blacks of the diaspora from each other, let alone from Africans in Africa, are unresolved within the political tradition that promises to bring the disparate peoples of the black Atlantic world together one day. Furthermore, the black intellectuals who have tried to deal with these matters have been highly dependent on European theories of national, cultural and racial identity. Du Bois's 1888 Fisk graduation address on Bismarck provides an interesting example here, particularly as Du Bois also admitted to styling his own moustache on the one that graced the Kaiser's face. In one of his autobiographies, *Dusk of Dawn*, he explored the significance of European history and its nation-states for his developing understanding of what a cohesive national identity for black Americans might involve:

> I was graduated from Fisk in 1888 and took as my subject 'Bismarck'. This choice in itself showed the abyss between my education and the truth in the world. Bismarck was my hero. He made a nation out of a mass of bickering peoples. He had dominated the whole development with his strength until he crowned an emperor at Versailles. This foreshadowed in my mind the kind of thing that American Negroes must do, marching forward with strength and determination under trained leadership . . . I was blithely European and imperialist in outlook; democratic as democracy was conceived in America.[10]

This understanding of national development and identity formation had (and still enjoys) a special appeal among the 'bickering peoples' of the modern African diaspora into the Western hemisphere. It has been integral to their responses to racism and directly inspired some of their efforts to construct independent nation-states in Africa. The idea of nationality occupies a central, if shifting, place in the work of Alexander Crummell, Edward Wilmot Blyden, Martin Delany and Frederick Douglass. This important group of Enlightenment men, whose lives and political sensibilities can ironically be defined through the persistent criss-crossing of national boundaries, often seems to share the decidedly Hegelian belief that the combination of Christianity and a nation-state represents the overcoming of all antimonies. The polymath Delany, who sets less store by Christianity than the others and is still routinely cited as the father of black nationalism, expresses this cogently in his 1852 book, which begins significantly by comparing blacks in America to the disenfranchised minority 'nations' of Europe.

> That there have [sic] in all ages, in almost every nation, existed a nation within a nation – a people who although forming a part and parcel of the population, yet were from force of circumstances, known by the peculiar position they occupied, forming in fact, by deprivation of political equality with others, no part, and if any, but a restricted part of the body politics of such nations, is also true . . . Such then is the condition of various classes in Europe; yes, nations, for centuries within nations, even without the hope of redemption among those who oppress them. And however unfavourable their condition, there is none more so than that of the coloured people of the United States.[11]

Richard Wright's later repeated warnings that blacks 'can be fascists too'[12] also spring to mind, possibly as a post-modern coda to this distinctly modern line of thought. As I hinted in the brief discussion of hip-hop culture, these problems of nationality, exile and cultural affiliation accentuate the fragmentation and inescapable differentiation of the black subject. The fragmentation to which they refer has recently been compounded further by the questions of gender, sexuality and male domination which have been made unavoidable by the struggles of black women. I cannot attempt to resolve these tensions here, but the dimension of differentiation to which they refer provides an important frame for what follows and I hope they will not be overlooked in our discussion. As indices of differentiation, they are especially important because the intra-communal antagonisms which appear between the local and immediate dimensions of our struggles and their hemispheric, even global, dynamics can only grow. Black voices from within the overdeveloped countries may be able to resonate in harmony with those produced from Africa or they may, with varying degrees of reluctance, turn away from the global project of black advancement once the symbolic political, if not the material and economic, liberation of southern Africa is completed. The open letter to Kwame Nkrumah which concludes Wright's important and neglected book *Black Power* is a complex piece of writing that seems to me to prefigure some of these alarming possibilities. Delany's 1859 *Report of the Niger Valley Exploring Party* (another text apparently excluded from the emergent official canon of Afro-American letters) is also germane to the dialectics of diasporic identification. Delany, who was a doctor, interestingly describes the sequence of clinical symptoms he experienced as his elation at arrival in Africa gave way to a special and characteristic form of melancholy:

> The first sight and impressions of the coast of Africa are
> always inspiring, producing the most pleasant emotions.
> These pleasing sensations continue for several days, more or
> less until they merge into feelings of almost intense
> excitement . . . a hilarity of feeling almost akin to approach-
> ing intoxication . . . like the sensation produced by the

beverage of champagne wine . . . The first symptoms are
succeeded by a relaxity of feelings in which there is a
disposition to stretch, gape and yawn with fatigue. The
second may or may not be succeeded by actual febrile attacks
. . . but whether or not such symptoms ensue, there is one
most remarkable . . . A feeling of regret that you left your
native country for a strange one; an almost frantic desire to
see friends and nativity; a despondency and loss of the hope
of ever seeing those you love at home again. These feelings, of
course, must be resisted and regarded as a mere morbid
affection [sic] of the mind . . . When an entire recovery takes
place, the love of the country is most ardent and abiding.[13]

The ambivalence of exile conveyed by these remarks has a long
history. At this point, it is necessary to appreciate that discom-
fort at the prospect of fissures and fault lines in the topography
of affiliation which made pan-Africanism such a powerful structure of feeling is not *necessarily* eased by references to the diaspora. This powerful idea is frequently wheeled in when we need
to appreciate the things that (potentially) connect us to each
other rather than to think seriously about our divisions and the
means to comprehend and overcome them, if indeed this is possible.

I am making a point about the type of theorizing we need to
develop and a point about the practical conduct of our political
lives. Both these aspects come together in the question of contemporary South African politics and they have a bearing on
how we might begin to consider the struggles inside that country
in relation to the tempo of struggles around South African liberation
which we conduct in this country and elsewhere. Here too, of
course, the issue of popular music as a vehicle for political sensibility which transcends nationality is central and unavoidable.

I want to make all these abstract and difficult points more
concrete and accessible by turning to some of the lessons to be
learned from considering the musical traditions of blacks in the

West. The history and significance of these musics are consistently overlooked by black writers for two reasons: first, because they escape the frameworks of national or ethnocentric analysis, and second, because talking seriously about the politics and aesthetics of black vernacular cultures demands a confrontation with the order of 'intra-racial' differences. These may be to do with class, gender, sexuality or other factors, but they provide severe embarrassment to the rhetoric of racial and cultural homogeneity. As these internal divisions have grown, the price of that embarrassment has been an aching silence.

To break that silence, I want to examine the role of black musical expression in reproducing what Zygmunt Bauman has called a distinctive 'counter culture of modernity'. The shifting relationship of music-making to other modes of black cultural expression requires a much more sustained treatment than I can give it here. However, I want to use a brief consideration of black musical development to move our critical thoughts beyond an understanding of cultural processes which, as I have already suggested, is currently torn between seeing them as either the expression of an essential, unchanging, sovereign racial self or as the effluent from a constituted subjectivity that emerges contingently from the endless play of racial signification conceived solely in terms of the inappropriate model which *textuality* provides. The vitality and complexity of this musical culture offers a means to get beyond the related oppositions between essentialists and pluralists on the one hand and between tradition, modernity and post-modernity on the other.

Black music's obstinate and consistent commitment to the idea of a better future is a puzzle to which our enforced separation from literacy and the compensatory refinement of musical art supplies less than half an answer. The power of music in developing our struggles by communicating information, organizing consciousness and testing out, deploying or amplifying the forms of subjectivity which are required by political agency – individual and collective, defensive and transformational – demands attention to both the formal attributes of this tradition of expression and its distinctive *moral* basis. The formal qualities of this music are becoming better known,[14] so I shall concentrate here on the moral aspects and in particular on the disjunction between the ethical value of the music and its ethnic significance.

In the simplest possible terms, by posing the world as it is against the world as the racially subordinated would like it to be, this musical culture supplies a great deal of the courage required to go on living in the present. It is both produced by and expressive of that 'transvaluation of all values' precipitated by the history of racial terror in the new world. It contains a theodicy but moves beyond theodicy because the profane dimensions of that racial terror made theodicy impossible.[15]

I have considered its distinctive critique of capitalist social relations elsewhere.[16] Here, because I want to suggest that its critical edge includes but also surpasses anti-capitalism, I want to draw out some of its inner philosophical dynamics and place emphasis on the connection between its normative character and its utopian aspirations. These are interrelated and even inseparable from each other and from the critique of racial capitalism.[17] Comprehending them requires us to link together analysis of the lyrical content and the forms of musical expression as well as the often hidden social relations in which these deeply encoded oppositional practices are created and consumed. The issue of normative content focuses attention on what might be called the politics of fulfilment[18]: the notion that a future society will be able to realize the social and political promise that present society has left unaccomplished. Reflecting the primary semantic position of the Bible, this is primarily a discursive mode of communication. Though by no means literal, it relates mainly to what is said, shouted, screamed or sung. The issue of utopia is more complex not least because it strives continually to move beyond the grasp of the merely linguistic, textual or discursive. It references what, following Seyla Benhabib's suggestive lead, I propose to call the politics of transfiguration. This emphasizes the emergence of qualitatively new desires, social relations and modes of association within the racial community of interpretation and resistance *and* between that group and its erstwhile oppressors. It points specifically to the formation of a community of needs and solidarity which is magically made audible in the music itself and palpable in the social relations of its cultural consumption and reproduction.

The politics of fulfilment practised by the descendants of slaves demands that bourgeois civil society lives up to the promises of its own rhetoric and offers a means whereby demands for justice, rational organization of the productive processes, etc., can be expressed. It is immanent within modernity and is no less a valuable element of modernity's counter-discourse for being so consistently ignored. Created under the nose of the overseer, the utopian desires which fuel the politics of transfiguration must be invoked by other deliberately opaque means. This politics exists on a lower frequency where it is played, danced and acted, as well as sung about, because words, even words stretched by melisma and supplemented or mutated by the screams which still index the conspicuous power of the slave sublime, will never be enough to communicate its unsayable claims to truth. The wilfully damaged signs which betray the utopian politics of transfiguration therefore partially transcend modernity. This is not a counter-discourse but a counter-culture that defiantly constructs its own critical, intellectual and moral genealogy anew in a partially hidden public sphere of its own. The politics of transfiguration therefore reveals the internal problems in the concept of modernity. The bounds of politics are extended precisely because this tradition of expression refuses to accept that the political is a readily separable domain. Its basic desire is to conjure up and enact the new modes of friendship, happiness and solidarity that are consequent on the overcoming of the racial oppression on which modernity and the duality of rational Western progress as excessive barbarity relied. Thus the vernacular arts of the children of slaves give rise to a verdict on the role of art which is strikingly in harmony with Adorno's reflections on the dynamics of European artistic expression in the wake of Auschwitz:

> Art's Utopia, the counterfactual yet-to-come, is draped in black. It goes on being a recollection of the possible with a critical edge against the real; it is a kind of imaginary restitution of that catastrophe, which is world history; it is a freedom which did not pass under the spell of necessity and which may well not come to pass ever at all.[19]

These sibling dimensions of black sensibility, the politics of fulfilment and the politics of transfiguration, are not coextensive. There are significant tensions between them but they are closely associated in the vernacular cultures of the diaspora. They can also be used to reflect the doubleness with which I began and which is often argued to be our constitutive experience in the modern world: in the West but not of it. The politics of fulfilment is content to play occidental rationality at its own game. It necessitates a hermeneutic orientation which can assimilate the semiotic, verbal and textual. The politics of transfiguration strives in pursuit of the sublime, struggling to repeat the unrepeatable, to present the unpresentable. Its rather different hermeneutic focus pushes towards the mimetic, dramatic and performative.

It seems especially significant that the cultural traditions which these musics allow us to map out, do not seek to exclude problems of inequality or to make racial justice an exclusively abstract matter. Their grounded ethics offers, among other things, a continuous commentary on the systematic and pervasive relations of domination that supply its conditions of existence. Their grounded aesthetics is never separated off into an autonomous realm where familiar political rules cannot be applied and where, as Salman Rushdie puts it, 'the little room of literature' can continue to enjoy its special privileges as a heroic resource for the well-heeled adversaries of liberal capitalism.[20]

I am proposing then, that we re-read and rethink this tradition of cultural expression not simply as a succession of literary tropes and genres, but as a philosophical discourse which refuses the modern, occidental separation of ethics and aesthetics, culture and politics. The traditional teaching of ethics and politics – practical philosophy – came to an end some time ago, even if its death agonies were prolonged. This tradition had maintained the idea that a good life for the individual and the problem of the best social and political order for the collectivity could be discerned by rational means. Although it is seldom acknowledged even now, this tradition lost its exclusive claim to rationality, in part, through the way that slavery became internal to Western civilization and through the obvious complicity which both plantation slavery and colonial regimes revealed between rationality and the practice of racial terror.

Not perceiving its residual condition, blacks in the West eavesdropped on and then took over a fundamental question from that tradition. Their progress from the status of slaves to the status of citizens led them to enquire into what the best possible forms of social and political existence might be. The memory of slavery, actively preserved as a living, intellectual resource in their expressive political culture, helped them to generate a new set of answers to this enquiry. They had to fight – often through the invocation of spirituality – to hold on to the unity of ethics and politics sundered from each other by modernity's insistence that the true, the good and the beautiful had distinct origins and belong to different domains of knowledge. First, slavery itself and then their memory of it induced many of them to query the foundational moves of modern philosophy and social thought whether they came from the natural-rights theorists who sought to distinguish between the spheres of morality and legality, the idealists who wanted to emancipate politics from morals so that it could become a sphere of strategic action, or the political economists of the bourgeoisie who first formulated the separation of economic activity from both ethics and politics. The brutal excess of the slave plantation supplied a set of moral and political responses to each of these attempts.

The history of black music enables us to trace something of the means through which the unity of ethics and politics has been reproduced as a form of folk knowledge. This sub-culture often appears to be the intuitive expression of some racial essence but is in fact an elementary historical acquisition produced from the viscera of an alternative tradition of cultural and political expression which considers the world critically from the point of view of its emancipatory transformation. In the future, it will become a place which is capable of satisfying the (redefined) needs of human beings that will emerge once the violence – epistemic and concrete – of racial typology is at an end. Reason is thus reunited with the happiness and freedom of individuals and the reign of justice within the collectivity.

I have already implied that there is a degree of convergence here with other projects towards a critical theory of society, particularly Marxism. However, where lived crisis and systemic crisis come together, Marxism allocates priority to the latter while the memory of slavery insists on the priority of the former. Their convergence is also undercut by the simple fact that in the critical tradition of blacks in the West, social self-creation through labour is not the core of emancipatory hopes. For the descendants of slaves, work signifies only servitude, misery and subordination. Artistic expression, expanded beyond recognition from the grudging gifts offered by the masters as a token substitute for freedom from bondage, therefore becomes the means towards both individual self-fashioning and communal liberation. Poiesis and poetics begin to coexist in novel forms – autobiographical writing, special and uniquely creative ways of manipulating spoken language and, above all, the music.

Antiphony (call and response) is the principal formal feature of these musical traditions. It reaches out beyond music into other modes of cultural expression, supplying, along with improvisation, montage and dramaturgy, the hermeneutic keys to the full medley of black artistic practices from kinesics to rhetoric. The intense and often bitter dialogues, which make the black arts movement move, offer a small reminder that there is a 'democratic' moment enshrined in the practice of antiphony which anticipates new, non-dominating social relationships. Lines between self and other are blurred and special forms of pleasure are created as a result. Ellison's famous observation on the inner dynamics of jazz uses visual art as its central analogy and can be extended beyond the specific context it was written to illuminate:

> There is in this a cruel contradiction implicit in the art form itself. For true jazz is an art of individual assertion within and against the group. Each true jazz moment . . . springs from a contest in which the artist challenges all the rest; each solo flight, or improvisation, represents (like the canvasses of a painter) a definition of his identity: as individual, as member of the collectivity and as a link in the chain of tradition. Thus because jazz finds its very life in improvisation upon traditional materials, the jazz man must lose his identity even as he finds it . . .[21]

By way of a conclusion, I want to illustrate these arguments further by very briefly bringing forward two concrete historical instances in which the musical traditions of the black Atlantic world acquired a special political valency. These examples are simultaneously both national, in that they had a direct impact on British politics, and diasporic, in that they tell us something fundamental about the limits of that national perspective. They are not, of course, the only examples I could have chosen. They have been selected somewhat at random, although the fact that they span a century will, I hope, be taken as preliminary evidence for the existence of fractal[22] patterns of cultural and political affiliation which will need further elaboration and detailed critical consideration. Both, in rather different ways, reflect the special position of Britain within the black Atlantic world, standing at the apex of the semi-triangular structure which saw commodities and people shipped to and fro across the ocean.

The first relates to the visits by the Fisk University Jubilee Singers[23] to England, Ireland, Wales and Scotland in the early 1870s under the philanthropic patronage of the Earl of Shaftesbury. The Fisk Singers have a profound historical importance because they were the first group to perform spirituals on a public platform, offering this form of black music as mass entertainment.[24] Their success is especially significant amidst the changed cultural and ideological circumstances that attended the 're-making' of the English working class in the era of imperialism.[25] In explicit opposition to minstrelsy, which was becoming an established element in popular culture by this time,[26] the Fisk Singers constructed an aura of seriousness and projected the memory of slavery outwards as the means to make their musical performances intelligible and pleasurable. The choir had taken to the road seven years after the founding of their Alma Mater to raise funds. They produced books to supplement the income from their concert performances and these volumes ran to over

60,000 copies sold between 1877 and the end of the century. Interestingly, these publications included a general historical account of Fisk and its struggles, some unusual autobiographical statements from the members of the ensemble and the music and lyrics of between 104 and 139 songs from their extensive repertoire. In my opinion, this unusual combination of communicative modes and genres is especially important for anyone seeking to locate the origins of the polyphonic montage technique developed by Du Bois in *The Souls of Black Folk*.

The Fisk Singers' text describes Queen Victoria listening to 'John Brown's Body' 'with manifest pleasure', the Prince of Wales requesting 'No More Auction Block for Me' and the choir being waited upon by Mr and Mrs Gladstone after their servants had been dismissed.[27] These images are important, although the choir's performances to enormous working-class audiences in British cities may be more significant for contemporary anti-racism struggling to escape the strictures of its own apparent novelty. It is clear that for their liberal patrons, the music and song of the Fisk Singers offered an opportunity to feel closer to God while the memory of slavery, recovered by their performances, entrenched the feelings of moral rectitude which flowed from the commitment to political reform for which the imagery of elevation from slavery was emblematic long after emancipation. The Fisk Singers' music can be shown to have articulated what Du Bois calls 'the articulate message of the slave to the world' into British culture and society at several distinct and class-specific points. The spirituals enforced the patrician moral concerns of Shaftesbury and Gladstone but also introduced a specific moral sensibility into the lives of the lower orders who, it would appear, began to create Jubilee choirs of their own.[28]

My second example of diasporic cultural innovation is contemporary, although it relates to the song 'I'm So Proud', originally written and performed by the Chicagoan vocal trio The

Impressions at the peak of their artistic and commercial success in the mid-1960s. The Impressions' 1960s hits like 'Gypsy Woman', 'Grow Closer Together', 'Minstrel and Queen' and 'People Get Ready' were extremely popular among blacks in Britain and in the Caribbean. In Jamaica, the male vocal trio format popularized by the band inaugurated a distinct genre within the vernacular musical form which would eventually be marketed internationally as reggae.[29] The Wailers were only one of many groups that patterned themselves on The Impressions and strove to match the singing of the Americans for harmonic texture, emotional dynamics and black metaphysical grace. A new version of The Impressions' hit 'I'm So Proud' has recently topped the reggae charts in Britain. Re-titled 'Proud of Mandela', it was performed by the toaster Macka B and the Lovers' Rock singer Kofi who had produced her own version of the tune itself, patterned on another soft soul version issued by the American singer Deniece Williams in 1983.

I want to make no special claims for the formal, musical merits of this particular record, but I think that it is exemplary in that it brings Africa, America, Europe and the Caribbean seamlessly together. It was produced in Britain by the children of Caribbean and African settlers from raw materials supplied by black Chicago but filtered through Kingstonian sensibility in order to pay tribute to a black hero whose global significance lies beyond his partial South African citizenship and the impossible national identity which goes with it. The very least that this music and its history can offer us today is an analogy for comprehending the lines of affiliation and association which take the idea of the diaspora beyond its symbolic status as the fragmentary opposite of an imputed racial essence. Foregrounding the role of music allows us to see England, or perhaps London, as an important junction point on the web of black Atlantic political culture: a place where, by virtue of local factors like the

informality of racial segregation, the configuration of class relations and the contingency of linguistic convergences of global
phenomena such as anti-colonial and emancipationist political
formations are still being sustained, reproduced and amplified.

Notes

I have taken the title of this essay directly from lyrics written and performed by
Rakim (W. Griffin). In his recordings with his sometime partner Eric B, Rakim
has persistently returned to the problem of diasporic identification and the
connected issue of the relationship between local and global components of
blackness. His 'I Know You Got Soul' (1987) was received as a classic
recording in London's soul underground, and since then he has produced what
I regard as the most complex and exciting poetry to emerge from the hip-hop
movement. The dread recording which directly inspired the production of this
essay is called 'The Ghetto' and is included on the MCA (1990) album 'Let the
Rhythm Hit 'Em'. I wish to thank my children for tolerating the repeated
playing of this cut at bone-breaking volume, Vron Ware for her insight and bell
hooks for the transatlantic dialogue which has helped me to frame this piece of work.

1. W. E. B. Du Bois, *The Souls of Black Folk* (1903) reprinted Bantam, New
York, 1989. See also the discussion of this in ch. 4 of my book *Promised
Lands*.

2. This phrase is taken from Wright's novel *The Outsider*, Harper and Row,
New York, 1965. In his book of essays, *White Man Listen!*, Anchor Books,
New York, 1964, he employs the phrase 'dual existence' to map the same
terrain.

3. Etienne Balibar and Immanuel Wallerstein, *Race, Nation, Class*, Verso,
London, 1991.

4. Nelson George, *The Death of Rhythm and Blues*, Omnibus, London,
1988.

5. I should emphasize that it is the assimilation of these cultural forms to an
unthinking notion of nationality which is the object of my critique here. Of
course, certain cultural forms become articulated with sets of social and
political forces over long periods of time. These forms may be played with and
lived with as though they were 'natural' emblems of racial and ethnic
particularity. This may even be an essential defensive attribute of the
interpretive communities involved. However, the notion of nationality cannot
be borrowed as a ready-made means to make sense of the special dynamics of
this process.

6. Henry Louis Gates jnr, 'Rap Music: Don't knock it if you're not onto its "lies" ', *Herald Tribune*, 20 June 1990.

7. I am prepared to defer to black Americans who argue that it is probably necessary to be both defenders and critics of the 2 Live Crew. However, watching the MTV video of their hit single, 'Banned in the USA', I found it difficult to accept the way in which the powerful visual legacy of the black movement of the 1950s and 1960s had been appropriated and made over so that it became readily and unproblematically continuous with the group's own brand of American patriotism.

8. Cornel West, 'Black Culture and Postmodernism' in B. Kruger and P. Mariani (eds), *Re-Making History*, Dia Foundation, Bay Press, Seattle, 1989.

9. Trey Ellis's famous piece on the new black aesthetic in a recent issue of *Callaloo* exemplifies the perils of this casual, 'anything goes' post-modernism for the black arts movement. It was striking how, for example, profound questions of class antagonism within the black communities were conjured out of sight. Apart from his conflation of forms which are not merely different but actively oppose one another, Ellis does not seriously consider the notion that the NBA might have a very particular and highly class-specific articulation within a small and isolated segment of the black middle class which struggles with its own dependency on the cultural lifeblood of the black poor.

10. *Dusk of Dawn: An Essay Toward an Autobiography of a Race Concept*, Library of America, 1986, p. 577.

11. *The Condition, Elevation, Emigration and Destiny of the Colored People of the United States, Politically Considered*, Philadelphia, 1852.

12. Wright's famous introduction to *Native Son* 'How Bigger was Born' and *The Outsider* include fulsome statements of this warning.

13. *Report of the Niger Valley Exploring Party*, republished as *Search for a Place: Black Separatism and Africa 1860*, University of Michigan Press, Ann Arbor, 1969, p. 64.

14. Anthony Jackson's dazzling exposition of James Jamerson's bass style is, in my view, indicative of the type of detailed critical work which needs to be done on the form and dynamics of black musical creativity. His remarks on Jamerson's use of harmonic and rhythmic ambiguity and selective employment of dissonance were especially helpful. To say that the book from which it is taken has been geared to the needs of the performing musician rather than the cultural historian is to indict the current state of cultural history rather than the work of Jackson and his collaborator, Dr Licks. See 'An Appreciation of the Style' in Dr Licks (ed.) *Standing in the Shadows of Motown*, Hal Leonard, Detroit, 1989.

15. I am thinking here both of Wright's tantalizing discussion of 'The Dozens' in the essay on the 'Literary Tradition of the Negro in the United States' in *White Man Listen!* and also of Levinas's remarks on useless suffering in another context: 'useless and unjustifiable suffering [is] exposed and displayed . . . without any shadow of consoling theodicy' (see 'Useless Suffering' in

R. Bernasconi and D. Wood (eds), *The Provocation of Levinas*, Routledge, London, 1988). Jon Michael Spencer's thoughtful but fervently Christian discussion of what he calls the Theodicy of the Blues is also relevant here. See *The Theology of American Popular Music*, a special issue of *Black Sacred Music*, vol. 3, no. 2, Fall 1989 (Duke University Press). I do not have space to develop my critique of Spencer here.

16. *There Ain't No Black in the Union Jack: The Cultural Politics of Race and Nation*, Hutchinson, London, 1987, ch. 5.

17. Cedric Robinson, *Black Marxism*, Zed Press, London, 1982.

18. This concept and its pairing with the politics of transfiguration have been adapted from Seyla Benhabib's inspiring book *Critique, Norm and Utopia*, Columbia University Press, New York, 1987.

19. *Aesthetic Theory*, Routledge, London, p. 196

20. Salman Rushdie, *Is Nothing Sacred?* The Herbert Read Memorial Lecture 1990, Granta, Cambridge.

21. Ralph Ellison, *Shadow and Act*, Random House, New York, 1964, p. 234. There are in Ellison's remarks the components of a definitive response to the position of Adorno in 'Uber Jazz'; see also Susan Buck Morss, *The Origin of Negative Dialectics*, Free Press, New York pp. 108–10.

22. I am thinking of fractal geometry as an analogy here because it allows for the possibility that a line of infinite length can enclose a finite area. The opposition between totality and infinity is thus recast in a striking image of the scope for agency in restricted conditions.

23. The radical historian Peter Linebaugh has recently discussed the etymology of the word 'jubilee' and some of the political discourses that surround it: 'Jubilating', *Midnight Notes*, Fall 1990. Reviews of the singers' performances in England can be found in *East Anglian Daily Times*, 21 November 1874 and the *Surrey Advertiser*, 5 December 1874.

24. John M. MacKenzie (ed.), *Imperialism and Popular Culture*, Manchester University Press, 1986.

25. Gareth Stedman Jones, 'Working-class Culture and Working-class Politics in London 1870–1900: Notes on the remaking of a working class' in *Languages of Class*, Cambridge University Press, Cambridge, 1983.

26. An 'Eva Gets Well' version of *Uncle Tom's Cabin* was doing excellent business on the London stage in 1878. See also Robert C. Toll, *Blacking Up: The Minstrel Show in Nineteenth Century America*, Oxford University Press, Oxford, 1974; Barry Anthony, 'Early Nigger Minstrel Acts in Britain', *Music Hall*, vol. 12, April 1980; and Josephine Wright, 'Orpheus Myron McAdoo', *Black Perspective in Music*, vol. 4, no. 3, Fall 1976.

27. These events are described in Gladstone's diaries for 14 and 29 July 1873. Apart from the singers' own text, there is a lengthy discussion of these events in the New York *Independent*, 21 August 1873. See also Ella Sheppard Moore, 'Historical Sketch of The Jubilee Singers', *Fisk University News*, October 1911, p. 42.

28. In his essay on the Fisk Singers in Britain, Doug Seroff cites the example of the East London Jubilee Singers of Hackney Juvenile Mission, a 'ragged school' formed after an inspirational visit by the Fisk Singers to Hackney in June 1873. John Newman, the manager of the Mission, 'felt that such singing from the soul should not be forgotten, and speedily set to work to teach the children of the Mission the songs the Jubilee singers had sung'; see R. Lotz and I. Pegg (eds), *Under the Imperial Carpet: Essays in Black History 1780–1950*, Rabbit Press, Crawley, 1986. Listening recently to my 7-year-old son's primary school singing 'Oh Freedom' in furtherance of the multicultural and anti-racist educational policies of the Borough of Islington was confirmation that slave songs are still being sung in inner London schools in the 1990s.

29. The phenomenon of Jamaican male vocal trios is discussed by Randall Grass, 'Iron Sharpen Iron: The great Jamaican harmony trios' in P. Simon (ed.), *Reggae International*, Thames & Hudson, London, 1983. Key exponents of this particular art would be The Heptones, The Paragons, The Gaylads, The Meditations, The Itals, Carlton and The Shoes, Justice Hines and The Dominoes, Toots and The Maytals, Yabby Yu and The Prophets, The Gladiators, The Melodians, The Ethiopians, The Cables, The Tamlins, The Congoes, The Mighty Diamonds, The Abyssinians, Black Uhuru, Israel Vibration and, of course, The Wailers, whose Neville O'Reilly/Bunny Livingstone/Bunny Wailer does the best Curtis Mayfield impersonation of the lot.

9 On the beach: David A. Bailey

A young black man, born and raised in the shadow of London's St Pancras station, embarks on a journey to Barbados, his parents' original home and his own home from home. There he discovers the real pleasures of recovering history and family intimacy. They cannot, however, conceal the deeper shock of his estrangement from the rhythm and the detail of Bajan life. What ought to have been scarcely more than a joyous readmission to the nurturing cultures of the Caribbean became instead an opportunity to explore the nature of his own necessarily compound identity. The superficial sense of familiarity produced in England by the simple fact of his Caribbean descent is not sufficient to give him guidance. It proves incapable of masking the realization that Barbados is yet another island nation where he will have to turn the distinctive condition of being in but not really of society, into a privilege. Transposed into an artistic strength, the precious but discomforting sense of distance and difference that defines him could, in turn, become a valuable vantage point from which important critical observations could be made and further historical lessons learned.

The after-shock of belonging neither to Britain nor to Barbados radiates out from these images but David A. Bailey's photographs do more than seek to make a virtue out of the inescapable feelings of cultural homesickness and homelessness that they invoke. Read through the imagery of the beach, the billboard or the schoolyard, Barbados is neither what England thinks it is nor what Bailey would like it to be. The church, the schoolhouse and the other core components of black cultural autonomy are all witnessed from an outsider's point of view. But the Bibles, the Sunday hats and the eager Brownies clustering around his camera represent the vitality of a Caribbean island still known as Little England, an island that remains perversely and ironically more English than England itself.

The clash of textures between the undulations of the warm, bright sand and the flat, gaudy surfaces of the postcards that temporarily and partially cover it, signifies both estrangement and opportunity. The viewer is invited into an extended meditation on the relationship between image and context in the construction and transformation of Caribbean identity. The piece demands that you focus on the disjuncture between the order of meanings that the Caribbean has back home in England and the meanings it acquires when you have found your own resting place on the beach which today constitutes its principal attribute. This is special ideological terrain.

For quite a long time now, the problem of developing an artistic practice consonant with the experience of being both black and British has been right at the heart of the work of the black art movement in this country. Everybody knows that this onerous task was produced out of pressing political conditions. Where racism dictates that blackness and Britishness do not and cannot be readily compatible conditions, the possibility of linking them artistically or demonstrating the complexity of their everyday linkage in the experience and imagination of black Britain rapidly acquired a provocative edge and radical potential. For a brief moment, to claim the right to be black and English at the same time was a gesture of insubordination crucial to the task of changing what England is. This phase may now be at an end.

David A. Bailey's photographs have addressed these contradictions in the past. Such concerns are still a primary component of this show, but it is also an attempt to move beyond them into a new mode, less concerned with critique and with answering contemporary racism than it is with the long, hard labour of cultural reconstruction. Of course, these pictures offer a contribution to the elaboration of a distinctively black, British sensibility. However, there are signs that this narrow obligation is now giving way to another even bigger task. It has become necessary to try to specify the limits of that distinctively black British experience while holding on to the idea that there is not, and can never be, an absolute essence of blackness. This is important because of the growing polarization between what can be termed the essentialist and the pluralist perspectives on black art and cultural criticism. The essentialist view has often been articulated through a simplistic version of what used to be known as pan-Africanism. Its popularity has grown recently but this is partly attributable to an anti-political, almost religious appeal. It is basically unserious about art and certainly incapable of discovering where the treasure of authentic black artistic sensibility has been buried under the rubble of racial oppression. This essentialist perspective is content with an politico-aesthetic outlook which minimizes the tactical difficulties arising from the black artist's impossible obligation to represent the racial community. Ethnic absolutism makes an entrance in colourful clothing but its authoritarian aspirations are betrayed by an open disdain for the diverse cultural choices and multiplex patterns of cultural usage revealed by the lives of black people in this country. The absolutist standpoint values a mode of artistic practice which can disabuse supposedly frivolous and ignorant folk of the functional illusions into which they have been drawn by the wiles of

Barbados beach

David A. Bailey at home in central London

white supremacy. The community can only be unified if its cultural life can be purified. Then its artists will fashion and donate a new racial consciousness capable of reversing the unwholesome effects of black dispersal in the West.

The absolutist perspective is often opposed by an equally oversimple pluralism. This has some virtues. It rightly affirms blackness as an open signifier and lacks the easy certainties that define its adversary. The pluralists are sceptical about identity. They can see myriad representations of black particularity that is always differing from itself and is internally divided by money and poverty, sexuality and gender, age and political consciousness. This inescapable multiplicity can even be celebrated if we accept the idea that the defensive drive towards racial essentialism is yet another symptom of our political immaturity. From this angle of vision, unitary community is both impossible and undesirable. Anyone wanting to discipline black expressive cultures according to their own particular desires can be confronted with racial heterology and repudiated on the grounds that nobody enjoys a monopoly of blackness. In theory, this is where uptight essentialisms yield to a more downbeat alternative. However, the party cannot start until all residual innocent notions of the essential black subject have been disposed of. An exciting blend of modernism and populism provides contemporary endorsement for the traditional polyphony of black cultural expression. No longer spurned because they are impure, the achievements of the black vernacular are re-evaluated. The profane strengths of black popular culture become an inspiration as well as a timely warning against aesthetic immodesty. This second tendency makes essentialism untenable by viewing 'race' as a contingent social and historical construction, but it has not always been sufficiently alert to the undiminished power of racialized forms of political and psychological identification. 'Socially constructed' should not mean insubstantial, secondary or trivial.

Each of these two approaches strives to answer the weaknesses it can see in the other camp. David A. Bailey is one of several artists who have realized the need to move beyond what is in danger of becoming a rather tired opposition. His bid to transcend the polarization of black cultural politics is directly articulated in the form of the show – in particular, the relationship between what he calls its deconstructive and documentary components. The formalistic, even avant-garde register of Bailey's recent work has itself offered a challenge to some fundamentalist ideas of what constitutes an authentically black photographic practice. This time, that formalistic impulse is refined partly through the use of colour and partly through the complexity with which the piece has been constructed. It is also tempered – toned down – both by its proximity to the relative starkness of the black-and-white images and by the obvious humour of the Caledonian Road billboard sequence in which the photographer himself appears. These very different kinds of material become emotionally contiguous. They are linked by Bailey's personality and by the different ways in which they accent their common referent – the Caribbean. They are neither alternative nor even complementary representations of Barbados, but rather contrasting frequencies on which the inner attributes of the postcolonial condition can be publicly transmitted. Brought together, they deepen and extend each other's range so that the viewer's attention is concentrated on the unique resonance of that postcolonial experience in English culture. This is notable because it is done without reifying a particular definition of blackness or succumbing to an essentialism that would foreclose what the black art of the future might need to be.

Thus the show points to a new range of possibilities. It speaks for those of us who, like the photographer, recognize that our lives encompass the histories of the Caribbean and the British Empire but are not exhausted by those histories or the unlikely configurations of identity that they support. It dares the viewer to join in the joyous, playful task of *creating* an identity which can contain the extensive cultural baggage of Britain's 'second-generation Caribbean migrants'. You are being asked to follow the footprints along the Bajan beach until you sense the shifting grains beneath your own feet. The post-colonial nomads must now learn to build the structures of their identity on sand.

10 Whose millennium is this?

*Blackness: pre-modern,
post-modern, anti-modern*

> *The silently growing assumption of this age is that the
> probation of races is past, and that the backward races of to-
> day are of proven inefficiency and not worth the saving. Such
> an assumption is the arrogance of peoples irreverent towards
> Time and ignorant of the deeds of men. A thousand years ago
> such an assumption, easily possible, would have made it
> difficult for the Teuton to prove his right to life. Two
> thousand years ago such dogmatism, readily welcome, would
> have scouted the idea of blond races ever leading civilization.*
>
> W. E. B. Du Bois

In spite of its triumphalist overtones, The Millennium Project
which is being celebrated here today has the virtue of raising the
relationship between the recording of history and the conflictual
processes of cultural politics. The opportunity for reflection
which it provides requires that we address the fundamental
issue of how to periodize the discontinuous strands of history
that bound Europe to its imperial subjects. Happily, the narrative
of occidental civilization and the myth of developmental
progress which are commemorated by this project are being

This chapter is the text of a talk given at a day conference to celebrate the
decade 1900–10 as part of a festive countdown to the year 2000.

systematically rewritten and rethought. The newly post-colonial citizens who dwell within Britain's well-fortified gates have been influential in this transformation. It is part of a long-term struggle to which works of art like Keith Piper's moving installation 'A Ship Called Jesus' contribute elliptically.

What I want to say this morning is offered in the critical and political spirit which such work helps to establish. This irreducibly political note serves as a reminder that we appreciate all that is at stake in calling this millennial celebration into question. The post-modern drift towards reading occidental universals as ethno-historical parochialisms means that the legitimacy of Western civilization and the integrity of its culture are perceived to be on the line. Whether they are really as fragile as the burgeoning debate over Eurocentrism and 'political correctness' in cultural axiology suggests, remains to be seen. However, in my view, there is little to lose in raising the stakes as high as we can and working to put the smug advocates of progress and rationality into positions where they have to defend their views carefully and with an intellectual rigour to which they have become unaccustomed.

I want to begin by querying the title of today's session: 'Imperialism and Modernist Consciousness'. The neat, binary opposition it constructs via those two pivotal terms troubles me deeply. It fixes both of them too firmly, both spatially and temporally. There is a suggestion here that we have left these two phenomena behind, possibly in the decade between 1900 and 1910. In cosily critical events like this one, we tend to be comforted by our ability to put the divergent things we are discussing next to each other and to congratulate ourselves on seeing their interrelation. We enjoy the dialectical transcendence of any opposition between them from the safe haven of our principled, post-contemporary pluralism. I want to ask if this sense of distance and the comfort it creates may be premature. The pairing of modernist consciousness and imperialism bothers me because it seems to encode the politics of 'race' in a modern and relentlessly Eurocentric topology which I also want to refuse. From this perspective it is unproblematically assumed that the modernist consciousness which really matters belonged to Europe rather than to its formerly imperial and colonial subjects. Similarly, imperialism happened somewhere else: out there in a remote and distant space. This is questionable for several reasons, not least because it accepts that the context in which our discussions will take place today is clearly and emphatically a post-imperial and post-colonial one. Both of these ideas are impossible to sustain in the once-great city of Joseph Chamberlain and Enoch Powell. Here even now, the vital history of the British Empire casts its long shadow over our discussions.

The power of these imperial dreams remains considerable, partly because they have been so forcefully repressed and so actively forgotten. For me, Peter Fryer's[1] brief and tantalizing archaeology of the relationship between Birmingham's metal industry and the trade in slaves opened a window onto a long-neglected area of English history which has the power partially to correct the national and regional amnesia on which contemporary racism has come to rely. Perhaps in our discussions later today, we can ask what varieties of modernist consciousness could have informed the fateful decision to trade guns made in Birmingham for African slaves 297 years ago?

Even if this pairing of imperialism and modernist consciousness is transformed so that it points to new continuities between the terms as much as any opposition between them, we still have to deal with the inference that as far as art and aesthetics are concerned, the cultural raw material directly and indirectly extracted by the imperial order was lying inert, waiting to be discovered, until some liberatory version of modernist consciousness brought it to life. The mythic narrative of civilization and savagery constructed here assumes that blackness – or some other 'Other' of Western rational man – lives in or can be found with the aid of the concept of imperialism, while the modernist consciousness which either confirms or contradicts imperialism was (and probably remains) the exclusive property of the West. What would it mean to disrupt this simple cultural symmetry? It persists even amidst the implicit recognition of nineteenth-century modernism's unequal exchanges with its colonial others. Something in the way it works puts blacks outside the West. Yet here we are, perversely up to our ears in it – being asked to enjoy celebrating its millennia!

The concepts – imperialism and modernism – are rather less authoritative, secure and stable than they appear when foregrounded by this event. There are also major problems in adapting the concept of imperialism to the requirements of cultural history. When and where was imperialism inaugurated? What problems does new world racial slavery pose for the coherence of that concept and its new sibling, modernist consciousness? What does imperialism comprise in discussions of culture, art and aesthetic value? How do we periodize its development, especially when its morbid residues so actively condition contemporary political culture? When, indeed, does a characteristically *imperial* version of modernist consciousness appear? With Caliban? With Crusoe? With Casement? With Burke's obsessive attempts to bring Warren Hastings to trial for his misdeeds in India? Maybe it commences with the fatal intermediation of capitalism, industrialization and institutional democracy for which the term 'modernity' offers a reasonable shorthand. Surely it does not begin with the aesthetic modernisms of the late nineteenth and early twentieth century which are best read as a repudiation of Enlightenment aspirations towards human social perfectability? In spite of the noble and critical intentions of those who put this event together, European imperialism did not begin in 1900, nor did it end in 1910.

The binary perspective on modernist consciousness and imperialism that I am criticizing offers blacks a stark choice. It locates us so that we live either at the West's periphery or in its interior space as the repressed, primitive counterpart to an undifferentiated modernist consciousness. At a certain point, this supposedly integral modernist consciousness discovers and takes its inspiration from vital, if not metaphysical, encounters with the 'primitive',[2] the tribal or the uncivilized – Flaubert fucking in Egypt, Conrad hallucinating in the Congo, Picasso visiting the museum of ethnography in Paris and Paul Klee peering at the Zuni War God in a glass case in Berlin are the archetypal figures here. I do not want to be misunderstood. I know that chronicling these complicated relationships is important; it enables us to begin to talk, as critics of anthropology like Mick Taussig and Jim Clifford have done recently about the connection of modernity's anthropology to modernist aesthetics. But – particularly after the MOMA primitivism debate[3] – this is not the only important political and intellectual agenda waiting to be constructed from the relationship of blacks, primitives, slaves, colonial subjects and other 'Others' to a distinctively modernist politics of representation. It should certainly not be accepted without thinking as the one true story of modernism's relationship to its imperial and colonial others at home and abroad. The effect of entrenching this narrative as an art-historical orthodoxy would be felt here today in somehow letting Birmingham, and indeed England, off the hook. Let me be blunt. We do not have to approach these questions via events in New York, although New York should, of course, remain prominently marked on the map that we make as part of comprehending them. We have to ask ourselves what a vernacular theory of the relationship between modernist consciousness and imperialism might look like. This critical political work has gone some way in France and in the United States, but it has scarcely begun in this country.

It is no less important to discuss what black and, in the context of contemporary Europe, minority modernism(s) might be. This is certainly not the preferred option within analyses knowingly premised on the imperialism and modernist consciousness duality. But it is raised directly by the Ikon show with which today's event is indirectly associated. Let me sum up by emphasizing that that duality misses a lot of what is important to me about commemorating the decade in which W. E. B. Du Bois first pronounced that the problem of the twentieth century was going to be the problem of the colour line. This was the decade in which the international pan-African movement began in earnest and in which anti-colonial and anti-racist political forces inside and outside the West began, tentatively and cautiously, to explore their potential political commonalities. Some of this was glimpsed fleetingly in the Universal Races Congress held in London in 1911. It may be one year too late for today's festivities, but what did Du Bois, Gandhi, Simmel and Thonnies say to each other? What implications does their coming together have, not just for how we understand the history of the imperialism/modernism (dis)articulation but for how we see the future of Europe and the place of blacks within it?

I want to pause over the learned figure of Du Bois for a moment. The first decade of this century marks the moment in which he emerged as a political leader. He was, rather unusually, placed in that position by writing a book – *The Souls of Black Folk* – which initiated a new mode of black political discourse in its deliberate polyphonic orchestration of various genres and voices. Art criticism, public and personal history, sociology, biography, autobiography, philosophy and fiction came together in that text to construct what he describes as the 'strange meaning of being black . . . at the dawning of the Twentieth Century' through a complex montage.

Du Bois is an important figure for many reasons. Certainly the emotional and political proximity to slavery that Keith Piper produces in his attempt to get us to revisit the hold of Sir John Hawkins's slave ship, would, I think, have been impossible without the indirect influence of Du Bois's pathbreaking historiography, exploratory aesthetics and sophisticated transnational political energies. He is especially important in this context because he initially crossed the Atlantic Ocean in the opposite direction to the journeys that his slave forbears had made. His nomadic life retraced the pathways created not just by the brutal triangular trade (with Birmingham somewhere near the apex) but by the different circuits of emancipatory abolitionist activity in which this city also played a worthy and significant part[4]. Du Bois knew that some of the most profound problems he and his peers faced commenced in being part of the West. He was clear that his associate membership of the privileged caste of Western intellectuals demanded that he strove to meet some special obligations. The first of these was the obligation to rewrite Western history. As part of the headmasterly cadre that ought to preside over the upper echelons of what used to be called 'Western Marxism', his work is bizarrely overlooked by forgetful intellectual historians of modernity and its eclipse. I find it easier to forgive this ignorance as a moral failing among the whites engaged in this critical project. It is not so easy to understand why it should so afflict blacks engaged in similar processes of archaeology. We need Du Bois very badly, not for any blueprint to be deduced from his writings but as a positive source of both provocation and inspiration in our contemporary labours. Du Bois is also especially significant because he came to Europe, travelling in England and Scotland long before the pan-African conferences were staged here. He studied in Germany for a couple of years and used his intercultural displacement and experiences as a global traveller to anchor his critical visions of where blacks might fit into Western civilization in general and American civilization in particular.

The drive of Du Bois's thinking from *The Souls* onwards, is towards figuring the history of blacks in a manner that calls the notion of civilization, and its attendant concept of progress, into question. He is also one of the first black Atlantic thinkers to try to theorize the relationship between modern consciousness and racial subordination – a relationship which, as I have already said, is not exhausted by the easy reference to imperialism in today's title.

Theorizing these complex questions at the junction point of his philosophical and psychological interests, Du Bois focused upon the double dislocation of identity and non-identity that he referred to as 'double consciousness'. The curious doubleness, which defines the distinctive position of blacks, inside the West but somehow not of it, is still valuable. Used heuristically, it can point to a more complex and wieldy configuration of the black subject than the idealized and reified conceptions of the thinking racial self that get too often and too hastily borrowed from Cartesianism and brightened up with a quick coat of ethnic or even Afrocentric paint.

Double consciousness and the theoretical apparatus to which it is attached find significant though melancholy echoes in the work of other dissident Western intellectuals, for example, in Walter Benjamin's insistence that 'the west is not the west'. It matters little that Du Bois is inconsistent in his view of double consciousness as an outright advantage. Sometimes he sees it as a gift of second sight. At other times, it appears as a disability – a process of splitting and fragmentation rather than an index of increase and authentic doubling. In either form, it still offers a valuable point of departure and certainly enjoys a strong resonance in the work of contemporary black artists in this country.[5]

Du Bois's innovative conceptions of modern black subjectivity lead neatly into his aesthetic theories which defy summarization here. His distinctive aesthetics insists (against the grain of modernity's attempts to separate truth, justice and beauty from each other and to separate them all from ethics and politics) that these three dimensions of human social practice should not, indeed cannot, be divided from each other.

> Artists have used Goodness – goodness in all its aspects of justice, honor and right – not for the sake of an ethical sanction but as the one true method for gaining sympathy and human interest.
>
> The apostle of Beauty thus becomes the apostle of Truth and Right not by choice but by inner and outer compulsion. Free he is but his freedom is ever bounded by Truth and Justice; and slavery only dogs him when he is denied the right to tell the Truth or recognize an ideal of Justice.
>
> Thus all Art is propaganda and ever must be, despite the wailings of the purists . . . I do not care a damn for any art that is not used as propaganda for gaining the right for black folk to love and enjoy. I do care when propaganda is confined to one side while the other is stripped and silent.[6]

This interesting example of what might be called a black Atlantic sensibility is one small illustration of the distinct modernist consciousness that grew in the uncomfortable locations inhabited by blacks in the modern world. The complexity of this history is such that it may require a complete revision of the relationship between the modern and the post-modern. It cannot really be opened up through the polar opposition between imperialism and modernist consciousness, even when we invert the relationship between these categories and reassign the label 'primitive' to the brutal antics of the colonizers. The descendants of slaves have known for some time who the real primitives are. This

inversion may be crucial but even this is not enough to understand the position of Western blacks, some of whom are inside
and against what modernity offers while others – Alexander
Crummell, Martin Delany and Edward Blyden, for example –
are not only inside but also decidedly in favour of just about
everything that the West can provide them with in the project of
civilizing heathen Africa.

I want to change tack now and point to a second area of difficulty which emerges in the bitterly contested space between
imperialism and modernist consciousness. This is a tactic regularly deployed in the everyday antagonisms of racial politics
which is common to both the vernacular and the more exalted
forms of black cultural production. I am thinking of the invocation of and appeal to the pre-modern as part of black artists' and
intellectuals' ethical and political critiques of the modern. This is
not just a way of reading the positive, celebratory enthusiasm for
the primitive that leaps off the pages of later work like Alain
Locke's 1925 anthology *The New Negro*, or animates the concepts of jungle to be found in black art produced by figures as
diverse as Zora Neale Hurston, Duke Ellington, Bob Marley and
The Jungle Brothers. I am thinking of the explicitly anti-modern
current in black expressive cultures. This denounces the advantages of modernity – its citizenship, formal political freedoms
and life chances – as a sham and is often part of attempts to
reconstruct the narrative of civilization's origins and developmental course. It is important to appreciate that, in this context,
pre-modern does not, however, mean uncivilized. Indeed, the
first essential motif which recurs in this enterprise is the appeal
to ancient Egypt as the source of global civilization and culture.
This was initially defined against the emergence of Aryan
Hellenism in the nineteenth century. It sought to provide an
alternative to scientific racism's account of the relationship
between the origins of civilization and the origins of racial

difference. This is a complex history that cannot be reconstructed here. Suffice to say, it would be a mistake to follow Martin Bernal's *Black Athena* too closely in seeing the Afrocentric account of the Nile Valley civilizations as just a residual, ancient explanation that lives on locked-in struggle against the characteristically modern cult of Hellenism and its constitutively 'Aryan' account of the process of world civilization. There is a sense in which it is a no less *modern* attempt to explain history differently. The symbols of the Nile Valley civilizations remain powerful not just because of the racist accounts which deny their African character, but because appealing to them has been institutionalized as a tactic which animates the ethical critique of modernity articulated by successive generations of black intellectuals. That is why people, even today, wear models of Africa around their necks. This is not just a strategy for reversing the polarity of domination and subordination so that Afrocentrism replaces Eurocentrism and the narrative of world civilization remains intact but is represented as black rather than white.

The memory of slavery is a second key to understanding the modernist gestures which blacks make in modernity's direction. I want to stop short of Keith Piper's suggestion that we have been sailing in the *Jesus of Lubek* ever since Hawkins journeyed to Africa. But the tradition of cultural politics which is being invoked, sees slavery as an *internal* component of Western civilization. Successive generations of black intellectuals have argued that it was not a curtain-raiser to capitalism, industrialization and modernization but a means to redefine their substance; as Orlando Patterson puts it, 'capitalism with its clothes off'. Of course, some see it as an anachronistic presence in modernity while others wonder whether it makes the very idea of modernity an impossibly utopian aspiration. But slavery, or rather the memory of slavery, and various attempts to make redemptive journeys back to the barracoons and slave ships is the second essential motif involved in the black Atlantic's critical response to modernity's dubious privileges. The artistic impulse to revisit this ineffable, sublime terror raises some pressing ethical issues. We should also ask how this artistic impulse is routinely practised as a form of vernacular cultural politics and history. An account of black music as a tradition of cultural expression would have to feature here. In the discussion which follows this session, we should also dwell over the hidden and not-so-hidden role of music and its expressive culture in making work like 'A Ship Called Jesus' possible. Again Du Bois is the first cultural historian of the black Atlantic world who presents black music as a mode of meta-communication that extends and transcends the limitations of merely linguistic signifying practice. Music and its attendant rituals provide the most important locations where the unspeakable and unwriteable memory of terror is preserved as a social and cultural resource. In music, which also offers a direct image of the will, a politics of fulfilment and a politics of transcendence come together in a modernist hybrid.[7]

Benjamin says that remembering creates the chain of tradition. His concern is with 'perpetuating remembrance', and here, this modern black consciousness shares something with his blend of Jewish eschatology and Marxism. They converge, for example, in a concern with dissonance, negativity, redemption and an aesthetic stress on pain and suffering. Looking at modern black art and the social relations that support it can reveal how this remembering is socially and politically organized in part through assertive tactics which accentuate the symbolism of the pre-modern as part of their anti-modern modernism.

This labour promises to illuminate the elliptical relationship between the modern and the spiritual celebrated by Keith Piper's installation. It is an important route back to the vexed question of periodization with which I began. Considering how the process of time is constructed and marked out publicly is the vital link between the ongoing critical work of black Atlantic modernism and The Millennium Project. The coming millennium will provide us with many opportunities to debate the writing of history and the periodization of Western cultural life. I do not, of course, want to exclude blacks from the celebrations but rather to explore, as successive black modernists have done, how the history of slavery can change the meaning of the West and the orthodox comprehension of its temporality, forever.

Notes

1. Peter Fryer, *Staying Power*, Pluto Press, London, 1984, app. F, p. 417.
2. Marianna Torgovnick, *Gone Primitive: Savage Intellects, Modern Lives*, Chicago University Press, 1990.
3. Hal Foster's essay on this in *Recodings*, Bay Press, Seattle, is a useful summary of this debate. See also Jim Clifford's brilliant discussion of the show in his *The Predicament of Culture*, Harvard University Press, 1988.
4. Vron Ware, *Beyond the Pale: White Women, Racism and History*, Verso, 1991, London, esp. ch. 2.
5. I am thinking of Sonia Boyce, David A. Bailey and a host of others who have addressed the double consciousness that arises in being both black and English.
6. 'The Criteria of Negro Art', *The Crisis*, vol. 32, no. 6, October 1926, p. 196
7. Paul Gilroy, 'It Ain't Where You're From, It's Where You're At: The dialectics of diaspora identification', *Third Text*, vol. 13, Winter 1990/1.

11 Climbing the racial mountain

A conversation with Isaac Julien

Isaac Julien, Britain's leading black independent film-maker and a prominent cultural activist, has adapted and reworked his controversial movie *Looking for Langston* as a performance piece for this year's Edge. The film, described by Julien as a meditation, cruises across a range of complex and politically charged problems. Among them are the construction of gay male sexualities around race, the night-time transformation and contested cultural meaning of urban space and, above all, the difficult relationship between the nascent political cultures of black Britain and their African-American step-parents.

The image of Langston Hughes, sometime poet laureate of the negro race, is used to mark and index some of these ongoing difficulties. Unsurprisingly, the film provoked an antagonistic response from Hughes's American executors and their legal representatives. This conflict has itself been incorporated into the core of the new performance. Isaac Julien spoke to critic and lecturer Paul Gilroy.

GILROY: *Both the movie and the performance versions of* Looking for Langston *elaborate upon themes raised by your earlier film* Territories – *how have you developed them?*

This conversation first appeared in *Mediamatic* (1990).

JULIEN: Yes, the links are in the relationships between territory and identity, territory and control, the spatial politics of surveillance. The *Langston* performance was first staged in the King's Cross area of London which has a reputation for sex and sleaze. Listen to the Pet Shop Boys singing. Because of the railway station, King's Cross is also a gateway into England, a doorway between north and south.

The performance used Camley Street in particular, a street that is notorious as a cruising ground for straights – it has a special geography. The proposed redevelopment of the area also means that there are certain political ramifications to the location. The whole space is going to be knocked down and renovated into a kind of Covent Garden yuppie village. It's barbaric. I enjoyed the idea of putting my audience into these different and difficult spaces where they might not normally go and certainly might not feel safe at that time of night. I wanted people to go into these spaces and to think about their architecture and its relationship to different dynamic forms of power – public and private, micro and macro. Making the film meant that I could expose those locations cinematically but actually putting people – performers and audiences – into these landscapes has a different kind of excitement. Talking to people after the performance, women in particular, it's clear that they took a certain kind of pleasure from just walking through those spaces at night and seeing some different things located there. Some people also felt that they were being constructed by that performance into the role of voyeurs. Some of them embraced this new vantage point, others were more uncomfortable with it. It's so different from the cinema! The audience are manoeuvred out of their passive position. They can also participate.

So there's a link with black vernacular cultural tradition too?
Black vernacular cultures have their own tradition of breaking

down the European division between art and life. It's not that
I'm anti the performance crowd but I enjoyed bringing some of
their high-cultural assumptions down to the ground. The idea
really came together in Camley Street in the shadow of the gas-
ometers. There, we had these two men walking towards each
other, both circled by a bright light. The audience sees this
encounter from the opposite side of the street and the traffic
flows between the two groups – performers and spectators. A
police car stopped and spontaneously involved itself in the
action. It was perfect. Even when the other people drove past in
their cars it introduced a kind of tension. My audience had to
engage with the occasionally intrusive presence of other types of
spectators. That was exciting. I liked that.

*You used certain features of that landscape – the canal, the
Coroner's court, the public gardens and the gay nightclub Traffic
– to stage the performance. What do they mean to you and how
are they connected to each other?*
They all change. They go from being public during the day to
being private at night. All of them host rituals, modern urban rituals which display things that are normally hidden from the variety of spectatorship that one associates with this high modernist
reputation of performance art. The performance format makes
visible the constellation of audiences drawn in by the memory of
Langston Hughes. It brings them into a physical proximity to
one another. That is quite unusual, particularly when you consider how segregated people's lives can be.

*How different are the black and white audiences that come to an
event like this?*
The dynamic in the performance was very much about white and
black and how I could portray the lived realities which specify
that some black and white people use these special places and

spaces to routinely transgress the boundaries that hold their racial subjectivity and their sexual identities in place.

It was particularly strange at Traffic. A lot of my gay friends commented on how strange it was being there with everybody from the performance. People thought the performance had ended and then the police entered (not real this time) and it was part of the performance too. That was very interesting. To a certain extent all of those places and spaces involve performances in which people act out new roles and identities. I wanted to invoke a gay sub-culture in which people think they are free. Those sub-cultural spaces are policed and that fragile freedom can be taken away as quickly as it came. It's the insecure nature of those sub-cultural locations that needs to be emphasized.

Isn't there a problem in being seen as a transgressor all the time? What about the right of blacks and gays not to be exciting?
In the past I called that the boredom of transgression. It's boring, it's a cliché – blacks are transgressive, gays are transgressive and when you put the two together then it gets really spicy. Who does this transgression excite or arouse? The different elements of the audience at the performance must have had different reactions. Some people thought that it could have been more provocative. They didn't read the performance as in any way transgressive and argued that it was rather conservative in fact, though others felt that it was right on the edge. There were three things that I was basically trying to do. One is to illuminate the necessary contestation which takes place over the memory, the legacy and the representation of an important black cultural icon like Langston Hughes. The second is to explore the possibility of having a sexual identity that many blacks would identify as a betrayal of their racial authenticity; and the third is to popularize some of the very interesting debates that have recently been happening around the history of black literature and cultural

expression. These exchanges, especially the arguments that have raged over the meaning and significance of the Harlem Renaissance, demand that we produce some new critical discourses different from those which have been associated with European ideas and writings. The Harlem Renaissance offers an interesting point of departure from which we can talk about the role of criticism in the development of black art or the intellectual tools we need to analyse a body of black cultural work. These are the same questions that we are having to deal with in black Britain today. *Looking for Langston* was an attempt to open up a dialogue within the diaspora on these issues.

What has the reaction to the film taught you about the topography of black identity? Langston Hughes was an Afro-American. You are a black man formed by some complex relation to England and Englishness. Black Americans have been deeply divided over the legitimacy of your borrowings from their cultural heritage. Do the legal difficulties you've experienced with the Hughes estate express the tensions between different national traditions of blackness and a broader diaspora sensibility? Put another way, should the film really have been called Looking for Isaac?

There is a sense in which the title was unfortunate, but I would defend it. Langston Hughes is important to me too. He is a symbol not just of the issue of sexuality within the race but for the experience of the black artist – the conflict between things an artist has to be and the things which are imposed upon the artist from the outside. These questions go right to the heart of how we understand cultural phenomena like the Harlem Renaissance. It was a very important point for blacks in America and for blacks world-wide. Black artists, writers and critics were working in a space which was segregated. It's extraordinary what energy all those people coming together produced.

Langston was, of course, the most famous and influential black poet in America. Reading the biographies of him by Arnold Rampersad and Faith Berry, it's impossible not to be struck by what has been imposed on him.

In terms of the problem of being both black and British, looking at it from the American side, there is a distaste for what they regard as a kind of mongrel identity. They think you're not quite African, you're British but you're not quite British and you dare to make comments about black America! It's almost like 'how dare you?' The tribulations I have experienced as a result of trying to show the film in America are relevant here. They raise questions of cultural affiliation and tradition through the issues of ownership and copyright infringement. These issues became a very important theme in the performance because they bring the idea of authorship into the foreground. In the court-room sequence there's a George Platt Lyons photograph that I've kind of appropriated and then you've got Mapplethorpe's photographs and a whole other thing about the relationship of control and desire. I would have liked to have used more of Langston's own work, maybe having some of the poems read, from a tree or somewhere, in a very Brechtian way. However, the pressure from the estate led me to cut out a lot of his work from the final version of the film and of course from the performance.

Are you confident, then, that the film and the performance go way beyond simply claiming a homosexual image of Langston back from the clutches of the straight world? Why should black artists living in Britain now be referred to the life and work of Langston Hughes?

When people say that Looking for Langston is simply a gay film, they are wrong. It's about black desire and the difficulties that engulf it. Similar problems exist with a number of other black cultural icons where sexuality is not the only or even the main issue. But it was at James Baldwin's memorial meeting that I decided that I had to make the film. The power of the official, respectable histories that can form around the memory of the black artist is something that I fear. Selections from Hughes's polemical essay 'The Negro Artist and the Racial Mountain' were originally part of the film and I'm still sorrowed by their absence from it. That text has an absolute relevance to the situation of the black artist today. It deals in a very powerful way with the autonomy that our position necessitates. That, above all, is the reason that I've done the performance. It expresses the need to celebrate, affirm and extend that independence. Hughes put it better than I ever could in the concluding sentences of the 'Mountain' text:

> We younger negro artists who create now intend to express our individual dark-skinned selves without fear or shame. If white people are pleased we are glad. If they are not, it doesn't matter. We know we are beautiful. And ugly too. The tom-tom cries and the tom-tom laughs. If coloured people are pleased we are glad. If they are not, their displeasure doesn't matter either. We build our temples for tomorrow, strong as we know how, and we stand on top of the mountain, free within ourselves.

PART THREE

Black Atlantic exchanges

12 Living memory: a meeting with Toni Morrison

In 1988, forty-eight of black America's leading critics and writers paid a public testament of thanks to novelist Toni Morrison. They were still grieving over the loss of James Baldwin. And mindful of the fact that it was only in death that he had been acclaimed as 'the conscience of his generation', they were determined to record their appreciation of Morrison's literary genius while she was still alive. Their feelings were galvanized by the conspicuous power and elegance of her latest and most accomplished book, *Beloved*. Her peers chose to express their love, respect and appreciation of it in intimate terms that contrast sharply with the marginalization of Morrison's work by the prize-giving literary establishment: 'dear Toni . . . you have advanced the moral and artistic standards by which we must measure the daring and the love of our national imagination and our collective intelligence as a people'.

Toni Morrison says that this simple affirmation of her work 'meant everything' to her. The unprecedented public appreciation of her writing underlined the political and literary merits of *Beloved* and is worth celebrating because it appeared in the hallowed, mainstream pages of the *New York Times Book Review*.

A shorter version of this chapter was published in *City Limits*.

However, the historic significance of this episode for black American letters lies elsewhere. *Beloved* arrived at a special and difficult time. The selective mass-marketing of back catalogue from black women writers like Zora Neale Hurston and the Hollywood-ization of *The Color Purple* had opened up a considerable rift in the black community. A bitter debate ensued over the gender politics of publishing black authors, over the relationship between black women and men and, in particular, over its disclosure to white audiences in cartoon-style representations on the big screen. In one graceful movement, *Beloved* brought these disputes to an end. It is a novel, not a manifesto, but it insists on an entirely new aesthetic and political agenda.

I asked Toni Morrison first about these arguments and about *Beloved*'s impact on them.

'Once you get into that geography you cannot get out . . . In trying to negotiate through all those channels it occurred to me that the male/female gender thing was either brand new or else it was made up or else it was good copy. It runs because it's a good story. It makes wonderful debates on television . . . Though there was some legitimacy in the out-of-context way in which some of the characters in *The Color Purple* appeared, particularly in the movie. Making it non-historical gave the wrong impression. They point fingers at one another, that's easy. Black men are subject now to a great deal of sensitivity about this, and they should be sensitive, because we can be easily manipulated. We can begin to use other people's problems as our problems.'

Morrison's work is continually focused by a concern with how blacks, living amidst the stresses of racial terror, can first acquire and then maintain emotional and sexual intimacy with each other. She has no fear of white audiences listening in to these discussions and defends an open approach to public debate of gender conflict.

'I write in order to enlighten black people, not from a need to explain to the others . . . I don't want people to say, what will they think about it if you write that way or if we have a movie like this. That means that we're still worrying about what they think rather than developing the discipline we need to communicate with each other. This is about me and you. When I write a book I don't have those people in my mind. I write what I think is of interest to black people. My criteria are very high in my books, very high because I'm trying to persuade and influence and clarify and examine and take on a journey black people. I can't talk down to black people. I have to deliver something real.'

Black women's experiences and, in particular, the meanings they attach to motherhood, are central themes in *Beloved*. For Morrison, these issues cannot be divorced from a different, deeper contradiction: the tension between the racial self and the racial community. This is explored in the book through a profound examination of infanticide. The story is loosely based on the real case of Margaret Garner, a young woman who killed her children rather than let the slave-catchers take them back to bondage. When arraigned for their murder, she simply repeated: 'They will not live as I have done.'

'It occurred to me that the questions about community and individuality were certainly inherent in that incident as I imagined it. When you are the community, when you are your children, when that is your individuality, there is no division . . . Margaret Garner didn't do what Medea did and kill her children because of some guy. It was for me this classic example of a person determined to be responsible.'

The Garner story illustrates more than the indomitable power of slaves to assert their humanity in restricted circumstances. It encapsulates the confrontation between two opposed philosophical and ideological systems and their attendant conceptions of reason, history, property and kinship. One is the product of

Africa, the other is an expression of Western modernity. Morrison sees the intensity of the slave experience as something that marks out blacks as the first truly modern people, handling in the nineteenth century dilemmas and difficulties which have become the substance of everyday life in our own time.

'Well, the people that we call the true modernists in painting knew the pitfalls of direct representation . . . The so-called modernist writers of the nineteenth century registered the impact of industrialization in literature – the great transformation from the old world to the new. Africa was feeling the same things. Can you imagine what it would have been like if they had left that continent untampered with? It's not simply that human life originated in Africa in anthropological terms, but that modern life begins with slavery . . . From a woman's point of view, in terms of confronting the problems of where the world is now, black women had to deal with "post-modern" problems in the nineteenth century and earlier. These things had to be addressed by black people a long time ago. Certain kinds of dissolution, the loss of and the need to reconstruct certain kinds of stability. Certain kinds of madness, deliberately going mad in order, as one of the characters says in the book, "in order not to lose your mind". These strategies for survival made the truly modern person. They're a response to predatory Western phenomena. You can call it an ideology and an economy, what it is is a pathology. Slavery broke the world in half, it broke it in every way. It broke Europe. It made them into something else, it made them slave masters, it made them crazy. You can't do that for hundreds of years and it not take a toll. They had to dehumanize, not just the slaves but themselves. They have had to reconstruct everything in order to make that system appear true. It made everything in World War II possible. It made World War I necessary. Racism is the word that we use to encompass all this. The idea of scientific racism suggests some serious pathology.'

With *Beloved*, Morrison aimed to place slavery back in the heart of Afro-America's political and literary culture.

'Slavery wasn't in the literature at all. Part of that, I think, is because, on moving from bondage into freedom which has been our goal, we got away from slavery and also from the slaves, there's a difference. We have to re-inhabit those people.'

The book is not a historical novel in the sense of *Roots* or *Jubilee*, but it deals directly with the power of history, the necessity of historical memory, the desire to forget the terrors of slavery and the impossibility of forgetting. 'The struggle to forget, which was important in order to survive is fruitless and I wanted to make it fruitless.' Morrison savours the irony that black writers are descending deeper into historical concerns at the same time that the white literati are abolishing it in the name of something they call 'post-modernism'. 'History has become impossible for them. They're so busy being innocents and skipping from adolescence into old age. Their literature and art reveals this great rent in the psyche, the spirit. It's a big hole in the literature and art of the United States.'

So why have she and other Afro-American novelists made this decisive turn to history? 'It's got to be because we are responsible. I am very gratified by the fact that black writers are learning to grow in that area. We have abandoned a lot of valuable material. We live in a land where the past is always erased and America is the innocent future in which immigrants can come and start over, where the slate is clean. The past is absent or it's romanticized. This culture doesn't encourage dwelling on, let alone coming to terms with, the truth about the past. That memory is much more in danger now than it was thirty years ago.'

Morrison is unusual among American radicals, black and white, for her consistent refusal to identify herself as an American. The 'I too sing America' option is not for her. 'My childhood efforts to join America were continually rebuffed. So I finally said, 'you got it'. America has always meant something other to me – them. I was not fully participant in it and I have found more to share with Third World peoples in the diaspora; may be it's for political reasons. I feel very estranged from black Americans. There are black Americans of all classes. Ralph Ellison is a black American and he's very clear on all that. When I say that phrase, what pops before me is a kind of bourgeois 'I have made it' person who is more foreign to me than a sympathetic white American who has never been a White Person to me.'

This use of James Baldwin's important distinction between people who make a political choice to be White with a capital W and those who merely have 'white' skin reminds me that Morrison was one of the speakers at his funeral. I ask her what she said and how she sees his legacy.

'I had been thinking his thoughts for so long I thought they were mine . . . There was a kind of courage in him that I have not seen duplicated elsewhere. Part of it is to do with homosexuality, with the willingness to be penetrated by the enemy . . . He was ruthlessly fierce and honest but had this tenderness that I never believed would last. He was this magnificent combination of manliness, courage and tenderness. How he arrived at that is still strange to me. Also, he did something with the language that nobody else had done. In his essays he has no peer. He gave me a language to dwell in. He cleared up things for me. His English did that. He was just able to say in six words something that had been confusing me for thirty years and I took that ability for granted . . . When Jimmy died, we had the drums going and they said "welcome to a new ancestor".'

Morrison's emphasis on the imaginative appropriation of history and concern with the cultural contours of distinctively modern experience make her harsh on those who believe that being a black writer requires dogged adherence to orthodox narrative structures and realist codes of writing. Formally, *Beloved* is a very radical book. She laughs. 'It's outside most of the formal constricts of the novel but you've got to call it something. Just as long as they don't call me a magical realist, as though I don't have a culture to write out of. As though that culture has no intellect.'

Morrison has located the innermost secrets of that folk culture in its music. Music provides a key to the whole medley of Afro-American artistic practices.

'Black Americans were sustained and healed and nurtured by the translation of their experience into art, above all in the music. That was functional . . . My parallel is always the music, because all of the strategies of the art are there. All of the intricacy, all of the discipline. All the work that must go into improvisation so that it appears that you've never touched it. Music makes you hungry for more of it. It never really gives you the whole number. It slaps and it embraces, it slaps and it embraces. The literature ought to do the same thing. I've been very deliberate about that. The power of the word is not music, but in terms of aesthetics, the music is the mirror that gives me the necessary clarity . . . The major things black art has to have are these: it must have the ability to use found objects, the appearance of using found things, and it must look effortless. It must look cool and easy. If it makes you sweat, you haven't done the work. You shouldn't be able to see the seams and stitches. I have wanted always to develop a way of writing that was irrevocably black. I don't have the resources of a musician but I thought that if it was truly black literature, it would not be black because I was, it would not even be black because of its subject matter. It would be something intrinsic, indigenous, something in the way it was put together – the sentences, the structure, texture and tone – so that anyone who read it would realize. I use the analogy of the music because you can range all over the world and it's still black . . . I don't imitate it, but I am informed by it. Sometimes I hear blues, sometimes spirituals or jazz and I've appropriated it. I've tried to reconstruct the texture of it in my writing – certain kinds of repetition – its profound simplicity . . . What has already happened with the music in the States, the literature will do one day and when that happens it's all over.'

13 Spiking the argument

Spike Lee and the limits of racial community

In a political culture which has looked, at least since the Harlem Renaissance, towards its artists for leadership, Spike Lee has been far more than a mere film-maker. His career is often felt to exemplify the trials and travails of black Americans in pursuit of autonomy and social and economic betterment. His triumphs and set backs have focused the aspirations of blacks inside and outside the film industry. Like the achievements of his sporting role models – Magic Johnson, Michael Jordan and Mike Tyson – Lee's activities have been endowed with a symbolic resonance that goes far beyond the original, artistic source of his notoriety. The reasons for this popularity, which is further fostered by Lee's visibility in his own films, are worth exploring. It makes sense to see his stardom as a product of the same catastrophe in black America to which his work is addressed.

Inside the industry, Lee's primary significance is that the popularity of his work with a variety of previously incompatible audiences changed the factors involved in calculating the cost–benefit equations of Hollywood's cross-over marketing. This shift has been largely responsible for opening the door to the much-heralded cadre of younger black directors. If they retain any progressive political interests at all, the other powerful and longer-established figures in the entertainment industry's black elite have chosen to pursue them quietly. Lee, who does not fit readily into the NAACP mould, has taken a different tack. His aim of politicized 'guerilla' film-making was proclaimed from the start. It was part of a populist pitch that has enabled him to reach into, and make use of, the most intimate content of black culture in ways that are unprecedented for a film-maker. Aside from an unbroken commitment to the tastes of the black public, Lee has bravely and consistently used his work both to attack racism and to argue that it remains a central structuring feature of American society – probably the most significant force in determining the opportunities that fall to blacks.

Outside the industry, there is something epochal about the way that black Americans have rushed to identify with Lee. His art and his activities as an entrepreneur are both important here. His corner-shop business schemes have put a stylish gloss on the old Garveyite adage 'race first and self-reliance', but it is in his more celebrated role as a victim of media racism that Spike Lee has become a star. His public persona – a difficult mix of victim and hero – has increased the impact of his work on the lives of African Americans at an especially difficult time in their history. The stresses of poverty, de-industrialization, militarized law enforcement, AIDS and crack cocaine have been largely unanswered by a system of formal politics which has proved incapable and often unwilling to try to change the terminal plight of blacks in US cities. This is a bleak situation in which the deepening crises of political leadership, ideology and direction in the black communities continue to take their toll. The strength of authoritarian organizations like the Nation of Islam is one symptom of this disaster. The rise of Spike Lee is another. Both give credence to the current African-American joke that the 1990s are the 1960s turned upside down.

Lee's unashamed populism has strengthened his work and cements its appeal. His black audience is invited to discover the pleasures in seeing its usually hidden and utterly segregated social and cultural world suddenly exposed to the legitimating power of celluloid. It is comforted by Lee's ability to construct recognizable images of racial community, particularly where the forms of solidarity in cinematic circulation are scarce outside the movie theatre. He has orchestrated the display of this secret racial culture very carefully. The pleasures of its reception actively construct the feeling of community that black political discourse often just talks about. The beautiful poetic recitation of great musicians' names in *Do the Right Thing* is one obvious and relatively innocent example of these characteristic appeals to cultural insiderism.

The inside cultural references with which all the films are overloaded are less problematic than Lee's celebratory attempts to be faithful to behavioural and political traits drawn from the same secret culture. His capitulations to the populist demand that black life be revealed sentimentally, therapeutically and without criticism have grown more frequent. The early films hinted at other possibilities. There was great promise signalled in Lee's preparedness to explore some of the divisive issues that inevitably arise to embarrass the claims of romantic racial rhetoric. Misogyny, homophobia and colour caste divisions all surfaced only to disappear, rather like Bleek's mother in *Mo Better Blues*, without being explored. The sometimes confused way in which they crept into view underlines the incoherence in Lee's righteous, assertive populism and highlights the ineptitude of some of his political judgements. His invented, abbreviated version of the black vernacular becomes nothing but a fetter when it prevents him from operating outside simple moralistic couplets. It is interesting to recall how, in *Jungle Fever*, Flipper Purify's pleas for complexity become progressively more ridiculous each time he utters them. Turning those pleas into an absurdity is one more clue that Lee's world is animated by a campaign against difficulty, complexity and anything else that does not fit the historic binary codes of American racial thought to which he subscribes and on which his allegories now rely: Straight and Nappy, Jigaboos and Wannabees, Bensonhurst and Harlem, black and white. Like Flipper, confronted by the horrific idea of the half-black, half-white children his world cannot accommodate, even though he professes his love for one of them, Lee wavers when he squares up to untidy problems that resist this logic of simplification. The internal divisions that menace the integrity of the racial community get played down or ignored. Old chestnuts like the responsibility of the artist in difficult conditions where that community provides strength and support as well as constraint, cannot be analysed. He retreats into the dementia of racial absolutism and its protective shell of masculine bravado when asked to consider the big, awkward questions like the way that sexuality, gender identity and male domination can fracture race consciousness. The bold idea hinted at in *She's Got to Have It*, that gender conflict itself might establish the intensity with which racial identities are held, has long been forgotten.

The complex linguistic and psychological codes that govern black popular culture are not always congruent with the more critical inclinations which Lee periodically claims for his work. This is confirmed by his (non)representations of women and by some downbeat endorsements of the 'Afrocentric' thinking which currently dominates African-American political debate. In this perspective it becomes impossible to criticize either the vernacular or Lee himself without confronting allegations of racial treachery. Lee is clearly most comfortable when meeting the joyous obligation to be affirmative or when engaged in sacramental repetition of the folklore and the prejudices of the ghetto he himself has escaped. Any conscious dishonesty here is less significant than the loss of an opportunity truly to uplift the race by estranging it from the corrosive conservatism of its taken-for-granted assumptions. These problems are most intense at racial populism's junction with anti-racist aspirations. Apart from a few rogue right-wingers, American blacks have sought to hold on to and even cultivate the idea of racial particularity as a salve to their chronic disempowerment. Through Lee's films it is easy to see that their protestations of absolute cultural difference announce their affiliation to rather than their disengagement from America and Americanism.

The youth cultural revolution prompted by the emergence of hip-hop during the 1980s has made the claims of black exceptionalism seem plausible. It has strengthened Lee's hand less through his close association with Public Enemy than through the notion that his film-making has been guided by creative rules derived from musical forms and styles. Lee's work has certainly redefined the limits of the African-American public sphere but the changes it has wrought in that sphere's internal character have undermined rather than enhanced the authority of music and musicians. Cinema has been moved closer to the centre of black popular culture and Lee's laudable and loving regard for that medium, refined in close cooperation with his director of photography Ernest Dickerson, has done much to systematize a new relationship between image and sound in an expressive culture where the encoded sounds of speech and music have hitherto constituted a specially privileged order of signification.

The problem of the limits to racial community has been inherent in Lee's work and in debates over its reception for a long time. The recent conflict over his newest project, a film on Malcolm X, brings it to the fore. In the current dispute, Lee's entitlement to make a film that explores Malcolm's life has been queried by political opponents led by Amiri Baraka who have challenged the film-maker's radicalism and his good faith. The waspish tone of this disagreement is one that Lee has himself fostered. As the icon for black America's intermittently absent father, as well as a model for the varieties of responsible masculinity required to solve its current crises, Malcolm was always going to be a hot potato. Baraka, who has accused Lee of perpetuating negative stereotypes, is on record as saying: 'We will not let Malcolm X's life be trashed to make middle class Negroes sleep easier.' It is significant that the main issue here is perceived to be class. It expresses the growing realization that, like gender and sexuality, the growing economic divisions and cultural and ideological differences inside the black communities mean that even in the United States there is not one single, closed and monolithic way of being, seeing, thinking and acting black. The same point is being made forcefully in the furore over Clarence Thomas succeeding Thurgood Marshall in the Supreme Court.

Writing about the politics of black cultural production in the late 1930s, the author Richard Wright described the evolving pattern of class divisions among American 'Negroes' and struggled to evaluate the way that those differences were being translated into different cultural and aesthetic forms. Wright argued that the choice available to the black artists of his day was expressed in a simple contradiction between the narcissism of a middle class that had dominated black art and letters between the beginning of the century and the Great Depression, and the great promise of unknown vernacular forms. The latter grew in a seemingly spontaneous manner from the urban black poor who sensualized their sufferings and turned the ineffable misery that flowed down the years from slavery into vital, if nihilistic, art.

Lee's popularity marks a point where this opposition could be reconciled if not transcended. His work represents the black middle class taking partial possession of vernacular style and expression, making them over, if not in its own image, then in the antics of the pivotal, heroic personalities that Lee inhabits in his own movies. Mars, HalfPint, Mookie and Giant are thus revealed as emissaries in a process of cultural colonization, and Mars Blackmon's afterlife as a Nike advertisement is the most insidious result. Through that character, above all, Lee has set the power of street style and speech to work not just in the service of an imagined racial community but an imaginary blackness which exists exclusively to further the interests of corporate America. Whether or not these streetwise products actually induce young black men to murder one another, there *are* unresolved moral and political questions involved in our racial heroes endorsing overpriced shoes, even while wearing a minstrel mask.

Right now, some analysts of life among the black poor calculate that, without three generations of higher education, black families will lack the cultural and financial resources necessary to withstand the pressures of de-industrialization and downward mobility. This bald statistic puts Lee's recurrent boast of being 'a third generation Morehouse man' into a different perspective. The economic and historical patterns chronicled by writers like William Julius Wilson reveal the fragmentation and separation of black communities into two divergent parts: a small black middle class which encounters prejudice in its competition with whites for a few professional opportunities, and a permanent, workless 'underclass' for whom racism past or present is secondary to the institutionalized effects of multiple economic disadvantage. You do not have to buy into Wilson's patriarchal solutions to this problem in order to recognize the kernel of wisdom in his diagnosis of black America's ills. The residual narcissism of the black bourgeois is still with us, although, since Wright's day, that class has gradually become parasitic upon the rich culture of the black poor. The hip-hop culture, which has recently taken the world by storm, is but the latest expression of the perverse cultural logic in which the most marginal group is also the most creative. The South-Africanization of cities like East St Louis and Detroit is the best-known example of what has happened now that this middle class has fled from the physical space it once shared with the black poor. It resolves its unwelcome position of dependency on them and their definition of racial authenticity by projecting a neo-nationalist ideology that entirely mystifies the volatile relationship between the two groups. The active opposition between them is thus dissolved in a dewy-eyed representation of kin, blood and communal harmony in which presenting race as family is the key to making the conflict between races and ethnic groups appear to be a natural, spontaneous and inevitable feature of social life. The conflict between racial or ethnic groups becomes part of an unchangeable human nature too. Lee sums up the consequences like this: 'Any race is going to say that their own race is a priority.' It is the fundamental symbol of the family which works to ensure that the concept of race is retained when the dimensions of the catastrophe in which it is embedded point to its overcoming.

Whereas the pathological family forms produced by external and internal racism are ruled by women, the healthy black family must be headed by a patriarch. The material horrors of life in America's urban black communities are far too readily translated into a panic about the vulnerability of young black *men* to institutional racism, poverty, crack cocaine, AIDS and the culturally sanctioned fratricidal compulsion to slaughter each other. It bears repetition that women carry the can for these idyllic, cosy representations of the black family. The politics of race played out as the politics of family is the background against which Spike Lee's work should be interpreted. His public projection of his own family is just the start. Dad, Joie, David and Spike himself are all hard at work uplifting the race. The deeply problematic and very tentative ventures into exploring gender roles in the first two films gradually gave way to a lyrical mode that might be called 'brownstone pastorale'. This idealized and relentlessly sentimental conception of stable, symmetrical black family life coexists with its antithesis in *Do the Right Thing*. It forms an ugly bridge between the end of *Mo Better Blues* and the beginning of *Jungle Fever*.

Of course, cultural play and racial affirmation are important. They can, for example, enhance black people's capacity to act as a community capable of defending itself. But aside from this, and the related question of morale, it is time to ask whether there is anything very useful in what Lee's movies offer us. 'Get your own pizzeria' is hardly a radical rallying cry. We may also require a strategy for dealing with crack cocaine which proceeds from a different premise than the notion that junkies are better off dead. Lee looks at the complex of fear and desire which has engulfed 'race mixing' since the dawn of America and, having explored the arbitrariness and absurdity of racial classifications, concludes with the absolutely conservative message that we should cleave to those who share our own phenotypes if the integrity of our cultures is to be preserved. Like Dap at the end of *School Daze*, Flipper is only able to bellow his incomprehending dissent from a world which has left him and his creator politically inert. The chaste, tender gesture towards the 'crack ho' at the end of *Jungle Fever* cuts against the grain of everything that preceded it. Lee is revealed, rather like Brecht who has influenced him so much, to be a lover of his chosen artistic medium whose loudly declared political commitments only end up trivializing the political reality at stake in his work and thereby diminishing its constructive political effect.

14 It's a family affair

*Black culture and the
trope of kinship*

The complicated phenomena which we struggle to name as black nationalism, cultural nationalism and neo-nationalism, have now been so re-configured that our essentially nineteenth-century, or maybe even eighteenth-century, understanding of them has to be abandoned. Everywhere, as a result of both internal and external pressures, the integrity of the nation-state, as the primary focus of economic, political and cultural action, has been compromised. The impact of this on nationalist ideologies (black and otherwise) is particularly important. I am not satisfied with just pinning the prefix 'neo' onto the word 'nationalism' and feeling that we've done the job of analysing its newest configurations. We have to examine the novel modes of information and cultural production in which the contemporary discourses of black nationalism circulate if we are to distinguish them from the black nationalisms of the past.

Perhaps the easiest place to begin this task is to think about the changes in information and communication technologies which have taken all nationalisms away from their historic association with the technology of print culture. This is one way of

This chapter is the text of a talk given to the DIA Foundation conference on Black Popular Culture; a different version of the text appears in the volume of conference proceedings, *Black Popular Culture* edited by Gina C. Dent.

conceptualizing the changed notions of space and time which we associate with the impact of the post-modern and the post-industrial on black cultures. If we are to think of ourselves as people whose black cultures and identities have grown from communicative webs that link several nation-states, how do we understand the notions of space and spatiality, intimacy and distance, raised by the writing of diaspora history? How do we adjust our understanding of the relationship between spatialization and identity-formation to deal with these technological changes in the dissemination of black cultures? One thing we might do is take a cue from Manuel Castells,[1] who describes the shift from an understanding of space based on notions of place and fixity to an understanding of space based on the alternative concept of flows. Or what an Englishman in exile, Iain Chambers, introduces in his very suggestive distinction between roots and routes.[2] If we are going to pick up the vernacular ball and run with it, then maybe the notion of the crossroads as a special location where unforeseen, magical things can happen might be an appropriate conceptual vehicle for rethinking the dialectical tension between cultural roots and cultural routes, between the space constituted through and between places and the space marked out by flows. The irreducibly diagonal concerns that grow from the desire to take diaspora interculture seriously suggest that the image of the crossroads might contribute something to rethinking the relationship between time and space in modernity and the narratives of nationality and location it generates. The crossroads has a nicely Africa-logical sound to it too. It is a point at which the flows of black popular cultures productively intersect. I have certainly found it a useful idea in reckoning with the impact of intercultural and outer-national processes that converge in London's black vernacular.

These issues point to the way that we will have to refine the theorizing of the African diaspora if it is to fit our transnational

post-contemporary circumstances. Although the current popularity of Afrocentrism points to other possibilities, we might consider experimenting, at least, with giving up the idea that our
culture needs to be centred anywhere except where we are when
we launch our inquiries into it. Certainly it means finding a better way to deal with the obvious differences between and within
black cultures. These differences live on under the signs of their
disappearance, constituting boundaries that stubbornly refuse to
be erased. I want to focus on the trope of the family and bio-
political kinship and explore the possibility that the growing
centrality of this trope within black political discourse points to
the emergence of a distinctive and emphatically post-national
variety of essentialism. The appeal to family is both the symptom
and the signature of this flexible essentialism. The relationship
between the ideal, imaginary and pastoral black family and
utopian as well as authoritarian representations of blackness is
something else that I think we should consider.

I wish I had five dollars for every time I have heard the trope
of the family wheeled out to do the job of re-centring things
every time the debates in this conference on black popular
culture have promised to question the spurious integrity of
ideal, essential racial cultures. The trope of the family is
especially significant right now because the idea of belonging to
a nation is only infrequently invoked to legitimate the essence
of today's black political discourses. Certainly in England,
and probably in the United States too, there are a number of
other legitimation strategies but the invocation of 'race' as family is everywhere. Its dominance troubles me because, at the
moment, in the black English constituency out of which I speak,
the trope of the family is not at the centre of our discussion of
what a black politics could or should be. I will return to this
point later.

The Afrocentricity that currently dominates black political

culture names itself 'systematic nationalism'[3] (that is what Molefi Kete Asante calls it), but it is stubbornly focused around the reconstitution of *individual* consciousness, rather than around the reconstruction of the black nation in exile or elsewhere. The communitarian, civic, nation-building activity that defined the Spartan-style aspirations of black nationalism in the nineteenth century has been displaced in favour of the almost aesthetic cultivation of a stable, pure, racial self. The 'ism' in this new nationalism is often lacking too. There is a sense in which the new varieties of nationalism no longer attempt to be a coherent political ideology. They appear more usually as a set of therapies: tactics in the never-ending struggle for psychological and cultural survival. In some non-specific way, then, a new idea of African-ness conveniently dissociated from the politics of contemporary Africa operates transnationally and interculturally through the symbolic projection of 'race' as kinship. It is usually a matter of style, perspective or survivalist technique, before it becomes a question of citizenship, rights or fixed contractual obligations. These were the things that defined the idea of nationality in earlier periods.

Although contemporary nationalism draws creatively on the traces of romantic theories, of national belonging, and national identity derived from the ethnic metaphysics of eighteenth-century Europe, Afrocentric thinking attempts to construct a sense of black particularity *outside* the notion of national identity. Its founding problem lies in the effort to figure sameness across national boundaries and between nation-states. The first sentence of Asante's credo *Nia: The Way* can be used to illustrate this. It says, 'This is the way that came to Molefi in America' but his text's elisions of African-American particulars into African universals belies this modesty. Look also at the moment in the same text where the author struggles with the fact that only 37 per cent of the blacks who live in the western hemisphere live in the United States. Forty per cent, he muses to himself, live in Brazil. What do we do about that? What input have the non-American blacks of the western hemisphere made into the totalizing pretensions of Africa-logical theory?

The understanding of blackness which emerges routinely in black political culture these days gets projected onto a very different symbolic landscape than it did in nineteenth-century black nationalism, in Garveyism or the nationalism of the Black Power period. The new popular pantheon of black heroes is apparently a diasporic one: Marcus, Malcolm, Martin, Marley, Mandela and *Me*! The narcissistic momentum of that masculine list is another symptom of a form of cultural implosion which must work against the logic of a national identity. The flow is always inwards, never outwards. The special truth of racialized being is sought, not in the profane, untidy world but in the purified psyche. I know that the triumphant moment of epistemological narcissism may be a necessary one in building social movements that actually move, but this post-modern discourse of ethnic inwardness abandons the world of public politics. It leaves us with a form of politics as therapy which is not, in fact, a politics at all and consequently has little to offer beleaguered black communities because it cannot resocialize itself.

Residual traces of an older rhetoric of nationalism do remain. They are there in the service of groups like the five percent nation and the Nation of Islam. But in the practice of these groups, these residues legitimate an ideology of separation which applies as viciously within the race as it does between blacks and whites. If there is still a coherent nationalism in play – and I say this from my own perch in London – I want to suggest that it is exclusively the nationalism of black Americans. This nationalism supplies a powerful sub-text to the discourse of Afrocentricity, but it has evolved from an earlier period in black US history. It is a very particular way of looking at the world which, far more than it expresses any exilic consciousness of Africa, betrays a distinctively American understanding of ethnicity and cultural difference. The family is the approved, natural site where ethnicity and racial culture are reproduced. In this authoritarian, pastoral patriarchy, women are usually identified as the agents and means of this process of cultural reproduction.

This is where the question of the family begins to bite. Representations of the family in contemporary black nationalisms appear to mark the site of what can minimally be called an ambivalent relationship to America. In recognizing this, I do not want to call it Afrocentrism any more. I want to call it Americocentrism. And I want to suggest that it has evolved, in a very uneasy mode of coexistence, with the pan-African political discourses which gave birth to it. Of course, the identification with Africa, on which Americocentrism is premised, is necessarily partial and highly selective. Contemporary Africa, as I have said, appears nowhere. The newly invented criteria for judging racial authenticity are supplied instead by restored access to an imagined, though not always imaginary, idea of original African forms and codes. It is significant, however – and this is where the trope of the family begins to look like a repudiation of the gains of black feminisms – that those definitions of authenticity are disproportionately defined by ideas about nurturance, about family, about fixed gender roles and generational responsibilities. What is racially and ethnically authentic is frequently defined by ideas about sexuality and distinctive patterns of interaction between men and women, which are taken to be expressive of essential difference. This authenticity is inseparable from talk about the conduct and the management of bitter gender-based conflicts which are now recognized as essential to familial, racial and communal health. Each of these – the familial, the racial, the communal – leads seamlessly into the next. Where was that heavy chain of signifiers forged? Whose shackles will it make? How does that conjunction reveal the impact, not just of an unchanged Africa, but of a contemporary America?

Now, the changed status of nationality in black political discourse can also be felt in the way that the opposition between the local and the global has been reinscribed in our culture and in our consciousness. Today we are told that the boys, and the girls, are from the 'hood – not from the race, and certainly not from the nation. It is important that this close-knit, resolutely local, 'hood stands in opposition to foreign things – if you remember John Singleton's film – in opposition to the destructive encroachments of Seoul-to-Seoul Realty. The same idea is expressed in Ice Cube's resistance to the idea of turning the ghetto into black Korea. Why is a rebuke to black Britain's Soul II Soul signalled by Singleton's choice of that proper name for the alien, Korean menace?

Observing these processes from some distance, in London, the untranslatability of the key term ' 'hood' certainly troubled me. I thought it marked a significant shift away from the notion of the ghetto, which has been eminently exportable, and which carried its own very interesting intercultural history that we should be able to play with. If the 'hood is the special urban space in which the essence of the new familial blackness can now be found, which 'hood are we talking about? More importantly, how do we weigh the achievements of one 'hood against the achievements of another? How is black life in one 'hood connected to life in others? Can there be a global blackness that connects, articulates and synchronizes experiences and histories across the radically local forms of black being that diaspora space now accommodates? It would be a shame if it was only the sign of Larry Fishburne-style patriarchal power that held these different local forms of blackness together. This matters not just because images of black sociality that are not derived from the family seem to have disappeared from our political cultures, but because, if Tim Dog is to be believed, Compton is as foreign to someks in New York as Kingston, London, Havana, Lagos, Aswz Cape Town – possibly even more so. Once again the naticate looks like an arbitrary point at which to pause our analpf the complex dynamics of black cultural production and Tim Dog's popular outrage against West Coast Gerri curls whack lyrics registers disappointment and frusiration that dea of a homogeneous national community has become impde and unthinkable. Maybe this is what happens when one 'd speaks to another, when incongruent, locally specific ideaaut blackness clash:

> uck Compton Fuck Compton Fuck Compton Fuck Compton
> Iaving a gang war
> ve want to know what you're fighting for?
> ighting over colours
> Il that gang shit's for dumb motherfuckers
> . . I'm Tim Dog and I'm the best from the east
> Il this Compton shit must cease . . .

Novo not pretend to understand everything that Tim Dog's perfance means in the United States, but in London it has veryticular meanings and effects. It generates a profound bewment about some of the more self-destructive and sibliidal patterns of sociality which have been a routine feature lack US inner urban life. That same tension between the local the global poles of black political sensibility – implosionne end, dissemination at the other – seems to be part of the r too. And, of course, when these things come down the tranional wire to us in Europe and to black folks in other partthe world, they become metaphysical statements about whackness is. We have to deal with them on that basis.

Ously there are other voices and there are other subject posis than the ones that 'Fuck Compton' constructs. One of the things I find most troubling in debates about rap is that I do not think anyone actually knows what the totality of its hyper-creativity looks like. I am a compulsive consumer (user, actually) of that culture, but I cannot keep up with the sheer volume of hip-hop product any more. I do not know if anyone can. There is simply too much of it to be assimilated and the kinds of judgements we make have to take that volume into account. It is a flood – it is not a flow, it is a flood, actually – and just bobbing up and down in the water trying to gauge its depth, tides and currents is not very fruitful.

If we come back to the family, the idea of hip-hop as a dissident, critical and oppositional space looks more questionable. Especially where the motivation of performers is constructive rather than nihilistic, the authoritarian pastoral, patriarchy of race as family gets reproduced. In order to emphasize this point, there is another voice that I want to present now which, in a sense, answers the calculated outrage of the previous one. It is an attempt, by KRS1, to locate the politics of race in what he describes as the opposition between civilization and technology. This is an interesting opposition because of its desire to hold onto the narrative of civilization and make it part of a grand narrative of black development. But this attempt is notable not just for its humanism – humanity versus technology – but for the extraordinary emphasis which falls on the family. I wonder how much it is the trope of the family that allows KRS1 to hold the very diverse forces of this new racialized humanism together.

> This is KRS1 from the mighty boogie down productions. Of course there is only one family and that is the human family. Beyond that there is a cultural family. I'm black which makes me part of the African family. Rise up and understand who you are . . .

> (Chuck D) . . . the Black man first must know who he is
> alright and then come to a level of coming to the side of the
> sister and both of them find out who they are and together
> working out some kind of situation with each other in
> community action to say that now O.K. we can both have
> family – raise children to be men and women.

I do not want to have to be forced into a position of having to
point out that it may not help to collapse our intra-racial differences into the comforting images of ourselves as brothers and
sisters, parents and offspring, any more than I want to be forced
into the position of saying that we do not *all* recognize ourselves
in the faces of Clarence Thomas and Anita Hill that adorn the
posters for this event – but the Americocentric obsession with
family brings these objections to mind. I recognize that the discourse of racial siblinghood is a democratic one. I know that it
emerged from the communitarian radicalism of the Church and,
as W. E. B. Du Bois pointed out long ago in *The Souls of Black
Folk*, this happened in a period before the slaves enjoyed the
benefits and the drawbacks of nuclear family life. The political
language of brother- and sisterhood can be used in ways that
accentuate an image of community as composed of those with
whom we disagree. From this perspective, the differences we still
experience in spite of white supremacy's centripetal effects might
be seen as a precious and potentially productive resource.
However, the wind is blowing in another direction at the moment.

Obviously not all of this popular culture wants to bury its differences in images of an organic, natural, racial family. I have
been especially engaged by the voices within hip-hop culture that
have sought other strategies for living with difference and building on the hybrid qualities of the form itself to affirm the value of
mixing and what might be called creolization. There are some
absorbing poetic attempts to explore the consequences of a new
political ontology and a new historicity. I am excited, for

example, by Rakim's repeated suggestion that 'it ain't where you're from, it's where you're at'. It grants a priority to the present, emphasizing a view of identity as an ongoing process of self-making at a time when myths of origins are so appealing. Sometimes that kind of idea is strongest where the Caribbean styles and forms, very often dominated by pan-African motifs, are most developed. Caribbean popular cultures have their own rather more mediated and syncretized relationships to Africa. It is also important to remember that reggae has constructed its own romance of racial nihilism in gun culture, misogyny and machismo.

This next tune I want to play, Rebel MC's 'Wickedest Sound' comes from London and points to a different notion of authenticity. Its racial witness is produced out of semiotic play rather than ethnic fixity; a different understanding of tradition emerges out of the capacity to combine different voices, styles and motifs drawn from all kinds of sources in a montage of blackness(es). I think that this version of the idea of authenticity, premised on a notion of flows, is alive in diaspora culture too. It is dear to me because it appeared within the specific version of hip-hop culture that we have produced in London. There are, of course, African-American traces here. Herbie Hancock's re-recording of 'Watermelon Man' is the most prominent of these, struggling to be heard among the Caribbean samples. It is a relief that the trope of race as family is audible nowhere. Instead we get a reaffirmation of black sociality based on the use to which the rebel culture is put. The old idea of a dissident, underground public sphere is being celebrated:

> Settle down for the new adventure
> Part two and this is the danger
> reality 'round the microphone centre
> so let me suffer them again mi selector
> now capture a lyrical lecture giving praise to Jah the creator

leave the drugs and clean up your structure
for the north for the south for the east for the west
for the black for the white
I cater

This soundtrack, a playful, vibrant projection of post-racial utopia, builds layer upon layer of black sound into a strong foundation upon which it becomes possible to argue that there is no betrayal of black political interests or cultural integrity in the acknowledgement of a white listening public. The ideal community being addressed is itself created in the act of using the music for pleasure and instruction. In the Americocentric alternative, a post-nationalist essence of blackness has been constructed through the dubious appeal to family as the connective tissue of black experience and history. Family has come to stand for community, for race and for nation. It is a short-cut to solidarity. The discourse of family and the discourse of nation are very closely connected.

There have been other periods in black political history where the image of race as family has been prominent. The nineteenth-century ideas of nationality as something that exclusively concerned male soldier/citizens were produced in a period when an anti-imperialist or an anti-racist political project among diaspora blacks was unthinkable. We would do well to reconsider them now because they haunt us. This is what Alexander Crummell said in *Africa or America*, drawing his theory of nationality and racial personality from the work of Lord Beaconsfield (Benjamin Disraeli):

> Races, like families, are organisms and the ordinance of God. And race feeling, like family feeling, is of divine origin. The extinction of race feeling is just as possible as the extinction of family feeling. Indeed, race is family. The principle of continuity is as masterful in races as it is in families, as it is in nations.[4]

This discourse of race as community, as family, has been born again in contemporary attempts to interpret the crisis of black politics and social life as a crisis of black masculinity alone. The family is not just the site of cultural reproduction; it is also identified as the mechanism for reproducing the cultural disfunction that disables the race as a whole. The race is nothing more than an accumulation of families. The crisis of black masculinity can therefore be fixed. It is to be repaired by intervening in the family to compensate and rebuild the race by instituting appropriate forms of masculinity and male authority. Even hip-hop culture – the dissonant soundtrack of racial dissidence – has become complicit with this analysis. It is interesting in thinking about the changing resonance of the word 'nation' in black culture that Michael Jackson has been reported as wanting to call his new record company Nation Records. (One of the things which is extraordinary about The Jacksons is that they have turned their disfunctionality as a black family into such an interesting marketing strategy.) Images of the black family complement the trope of family that appears in the cultural forms themselves. They are all around us in the selling of black popular culture. They are so visible in the marketing of Spike Lee and his projects that they point to the value of reading his oeuvre as a succession of Oedipal crises.

On the strange kind of cultural loop I live, I saw Marlon Riggs's powerful film *Tongues Untied* for the second time on the same night that I first saw *Boyz in the 'Hood* (we get these things in a different sequence than you do). Listening to that authoritative voice saying that black men loving black men was *the* revolutionary act – not *a* revolutionary act but *the* revolutionary act – the force of that definite article set me to thinking about *Boyz in the 'Hood* too. I know there are differences. I have an idea of where some of them dwell. But are there not also similarities and convergences in the way that love between men is the common focus of these 'texts'?

Let me begin to sum up by saying why I think the prominence of the family is a problem. Spreading the Oedipal narrative around a bit can probably produce some interesting effects. But it bears repetition that the trope of family is central to the means whereby the crisis that we are living – of black social and political life – gets exclusively represented as the crisis of black masculinity. It is there, also, in the way that conflict, within our communities and between our communities, gets resolved through the mystic reconstruction of an ideal heterosexual family. This is the oldest conservative device in the book of modern culture. Once again, *Boyz in the 'Hood* is the most obvious illustration of an authentically black and supposedly radical product that is complacently comfortable working within those deeply conservative codes. In Isaac Julien's recent black British film *Young Soul Rebels*, there is a fragile image of non-familial community which appears and has been much criticized. It is the point at which the film ends and a kind of surrogate, joyfully disorganic and synthetic kin group constitutes itself slowly and tentatively – in and around transgressive phenotypically asymmetrical desire, through music, affirmation, celebration and play.

Lest this look like a binary split between conservative, familial Americana and the transgressive counter-culture of black Britons, I want to amplify what I take to be a similar note of disorganicity in the way that kinship can be represented which is drawn from an American hip-hop record popular on both sides of the Atlantic right now. It is a tune called 'Be a Father to Your Child' by Ed O.G. and The Bulldogs. It has been very popular in London, partly because of the sample it uses – a black nationalist love song called 'Searching' which was written and performed by Roy Ayers in the 1970s. The earlier cut gets transposed into a different conceptual key by the contemporary appropriation. There are two things that have interested me about this tune.

First of all, the object of desire in the original version was clearly gendered female. The original is about searching for the love of a black woman. In the Ed O.G. version, the object of desire is ungendered. I found the opening up of that signifier suggestive. It means that when Ed O.G. talks about familial obligation, he is not saying be a father to your son – he is saying be a father to your child. Second, and more importantly, he makes the pragmatic *functionality* of family the decisive issue. This is not the biological payback involved in family life. If you are responsible for producing a child with someone, he says, and that child is being supported by somebody else who is prepared to father it effectively when you fail, even if that person is not the biological parent, then back off and let them get on with it. That small gesture was something I wanted to celebrate. I think it shows – although I do not want to sound prescriptive about this – that the struggle over the meaning of family is alive within the culture, that a critical perspective on these big complex questions is not something which needs to be imported into that vernacular from outside by people like us. We should not be so immodest as to imagine we can play that role.

> how would you like it if your father was a stranger
> and then tried to come into your life and tried to change
> the way your mother raised ya?
> now wouldn't that amaze ya?
> to be or not to be that is the question
> when you're wrong you're wrong
> it's hard to make a correction
> harassing the woman for being with another man
> but if the brother man can do it better than you can
> let him
> don't sweat him
> let him do the job that you couldn't do
> you're claiming you were there, but not when she needed you

and now you want to come around for a day or two
it's never too late to correct your mistakes
and be a father to your child

I'll end by saying that even the best of this discourse of the familialization of politics is still a problem. I do not want to lose sight of that. I want to have it both ways. I want to be able to valorize what we can recover, but also to cite the disastrous consequences that follow when the family supplies the only symbols of political agency we can find in the culture and the only object upon which that agency can be seen to operate. Let us remind ourselves that there are other possibilities. Historically, black political culture's most powerful notions of agency have been figured through the sacred. They can also get figured through the profane where a different utopia and idea of worldly redemption can be observed. Both of these possibilities come together for me in the traditions of musical performance that culminate in hiphop. There, we find what I call the ethics of antiphony – a kind of ideal communicative moment in the relationship between the performer and the crowd which surpasses anything the structures of the family can provide.

Notes

1. *The Informational City*, Basil Blackwell, Oxford, 1991.
2. This distinction has been employed in similar ways by Dick Hebdige and James Clifford. See Chambers's *Border Dialogues*, Routledge, London, 1990.
3. Molefi Kete Asante, *Afrocentricity*, Africa World Press, Trenton, NJ, 1988.
4. *Africa or America*, Willey, Springfield, MA, p 46.

15 A dialogue with bell hooks

BELL HOOKS One of the things I have enjoyed since I met you and started reading your work is thinking about the idea of the black Atlantic world. Are you the only person who uses that term?

PAUL GILROY No, it's a term that I took from reading some of the debates about African art history and the relationship between the recognizably African cultures in the western hemisphere and the West African cultures from which they partially stem. It's a term that I associate with the work of some rather conventional historians of African art though it also appears in some of the more sensitive histories of mercantilism. I borrowed it because I wanted to supplement the diaspora idea with a concept that emphasized the in-between and the intercultural. In art history, the term is about cultural affiliation and connection but it is exclusively a one-way process stemming from Africa and pointing westwards. I wanted to change the concept so that it could address other connections that moved in the opposite direction and made them part of the story too.

This conversation took place in London during the summer of 1992.

BELL HOOKS It's interesting because I think that a lot of black scholars really haven't paid very much attention to art as a space in diasporic black experience where one can trace continuities. In the United States that is the domain of predominantly white art historians. I think it's changing now but it's interesting. I was thinking about that because of the discussions we've been having about Afrocentrism. There's really no discussion of art and the place of art in the discussions about identity that have been produced by the new black nationalism. It's a very different kind of black nationalism from that of the 1960s. That nationalism really saw art and culture as a special place. These days there's a very, very dry sense of culture.

PAUL GILROY I think that's right. It's austere. I notice it most of all in the complete silence in that whole body of work about popular culture. There's nothing being said about popular culture there. I wonder why that is? I wonder if it's because, to talk about popular culture, one has to confront the whole 'contamination' of supposedly pure African forms. Africa provided the critical substance for that process of mutation and adaptation we call creolization. The serious study of black popular culture affirms that intermixture in some way. If you want to repudiate that process of adaptation and growth and are trying in its place to reconstruct some notion of a purified African culture, you have to stay clear of the vernacular. Investigating the black Atlantic diaspora means that you have to reckon with the creolization process as a founding moment, a point in time when new relations, cultures and conflicts were brought into being.

BELL HOOKS We've been talking a lot about ways that some of the more prominent strands of Afrocentrism in the States really mirror certain white Western philosophical ways of thinking about the self. I was thinking in response to the comment you just

made about how much there's an insistence in Afrocentric thinking on the importance of high culture. So it's more than just an
absence of discussion about popular culture. Afrocentrism
reproduces certain white bourgeois assumptions. The only cultural space that's valued is the space held by science. Part of the
big focus on ancient Egypt is this idea to sort of reinvent black
people as the people who did the hard sciences . . .

PAUL GILROY A stolen legacy, that's where the arguments about
anteriority begin to bite. You're right about the self. But there's
also a whole sense of time and history at work which is quite distinctly European. Blacks can become complicit with it. A lot of
the time it looks as if the great narrative of civilization's development isn't in itself a problem, all that matters is our title to it.

BELL HOOKS It's interesting how Afrocentrism is very different
from the type of reclamation of history that someone like Ivan
van Sertima is working with because he isn't trying to recover an
unproblematic black history in which you just say 'we were
wonderful, we were great'. In his approach, you're able to ask
questions about who these Africans were who were meeting
native Americans. It's not made to seem like this wonderful
world of great Africans. A real distinction has to be made
between the work of people like van Sertima and Jan Carew in
making those connections between different groups: native
Americans, Africans and others and that mythic construction of
Africa that's at the centre of some contemporary Afrocentric
thinking.

PAUL GILROY There are two points that I want to take up. Firstly,
we have to be careful that in our political critique of Afrocentrism we don't overlook the need to be affirmative and sometimes to be able to say these things were great and wonderful.

The ability to take pleasure in them, I think that's important. But a bigger issue is how we get prevented and prevent ourselves from saying 'well yes, this was great, but there were also these problems with it'.

BELL HOOKS I think that shows again one of the things I have been thinking a lot about in the last few years: how deeply Western some African Americans are. We see those Western sensibilities come out in the construction of how we want to re-evoke and remember Africa. In some ways it's a very nineteenth-century way of thinking, a reflection of the ways in which the West has always remembered Africa nostalgically. I don't see it as a break with dominant ways that Africa has been viewed. It doesn't fall into this neat thing that white people have viewed Africa negatively, because if we are really going to talk about historical representations of Africa then we have to talk about that whole strand of whiteness that didn't view Africa as negative at all but viewed it as part of this harmonious, natural world that to some extent resembles what Afrocentric thinkers are evoking. I always think of this when people say to me 'We don't need feminism because if we return to our African roots we'll find that there was gender equity.'

PAUL GILROY That state of being closer to nature is seen as a state of simple bliss. It gets connected to an argument about individuality and the desirability of finding harmony by being dissolved into the general will. This type of Afrocentric thinking is a bit like Rousseau, isn't it?

BELL HOOKS Very much like Rousseau. That has been the hardest thing for me in discussions about Afrocentrism in the United States. People want to deny that, however oppressed black people have been and still are in the United States, there is still this very deep Western sensibility that isn't necessarily Eurocentric in the sense of buying into the idea of whiteness as better, but is philosophically very bound to Western codes and conventions. You have talked about the Cartesian sense of the self and the will and pointed out how similar Afrocentrism is to that. I was just so struck by Shaharazad Ali's book *The Black Man's Guide to Understanding the Black Woman* because so much of what was in that book seemed to have been lifted out of eighteenth- and nineteenth-century manuals of the proper decorum and behaviour between the genders.

PAUL GILROY The ideas of Rousseau are an important key to Afrocentrism, not just because of that ideal image of the blissful community that he offers but because in his work that model gets mixed with another way of understanding social life, community and citizenship. The second element is drawn from his understanding of the history of Sparta. The Spartan sense of community and citizenship provided him with a model in which the public sphere is male and where the household is an opaque space for the reproduction of the culture. I find it odd that these habits of mind still have such a hold among people who have had such immediate experiences of the barbarism that those ideas can create. I am very interested in the way that the Africa that is the object of these discourses is not *contemporary* Africa at all! It may be that this is an effect of my location in Europe, but from that distance I don't hear American Afrocentrics saying anything at all about the problem of debt or the ecological crisis in Africa. Where they talk about things like the question of AIDS in Africa, for example, they don't say anything about the practical political problems it raises. Maybe this will have to change. I wonder what kind of a relationship is looked for between their Afrocentric commitment which is real and speaks to the real needs of the exile, and the plight of Africa in the next decade and the next century. What kind of political connections are we missing here? What sort of opportunities are being spurned? What will happen when the experiential and political gulf between Africans in Africa and blacks in the western hemisphere is even deeper and wider than it is now? Do you think that black Americans or blacks in Europe will want to go on identifying with Africa?

BELL HOOKS I don't feel like I hear an identification with a real Africa, an Africa that has a history but is also contemporary. In coming to terms with a contemporary Africa one has to deconstruct the sense of blackness as associated only with goodness. We have to consider the association of blackness with forms of fascism and corruption, for example. That's why the politics of contemporary Africa make it very hard for many Afrocentric thinkers to confront that Africa at all. Just recently I was at a talk where I was saying to people, what will it mean for black Americans to try to get in touch with an Africa that means we have to learn? We will have to read and study and approach the various cultures and histories of Africa with more than just a nostalgic or sentimental identification but one that says that Africa is not simple. To understand Africa one has to cultivate and apply vigilant and critical thought. I don't see anywhere in the States a large sort of awakening of this sense of Africa. In the writing of people like Na'im Akbar, or Karenga and Molefi Asante, I noticed that there's been very little attempt to incorporate Malcolm X into the way that their Afrocentrisms are constructed. I think this has a lot to do with the global political awareness that was happening towards the end of Malcolm's life. That binary opposition between blackness and whiteness that had characterized so much of his earlier, polemical messages began to disappear. There was a recognition on his part that Africa is a complex place and that the notion of race had to be thought of differently when one thinks about a continent that is as large and diverse as Africa. In a way, sometimes I feel that the Afrocentric thinkers haven't any need for Malcolm. Even the neo-nationalism in the States still refuses to see that the Malcolm it wants to claim is really the early Malcolm, a Malcolm that is totally rooted in those binary conceptions that derive from American history. I feel that this is another deep mark of the profound political crisis of African Americans. It seems that we don't collectively have the political skills to respond to contemporary pressures. When people are in that position they have to come up with a different survival strategy. But our strategy seems to be rooted in the need to have a romantic escape, a vision of Africa that is like a cartoon in the sense that it offers us superheroes. Isis and Osiris are reconstructed as black superheroes but this has no relation to our actual political needs or to the needs of Africa.

PAUL GILROY I understand that. I began to realize that we had to think about these things in a different way when I visited Egypt. I noticed the tour parties of African Americans wandering around in places like the Valley of the Kings and the museum in Cairo. I tried to engage these people in conversation precisely about the pleasure we were all getting in being immersed in that awesome history and about the ways we could see that it had been made over in a historiography which was not in the interests of black people and had had terrible consequences. I was also interested in the recovery of a counter-history as contested social memory. I felt a bit saddened about the reluctance or inability of the black Americans I met to be reflexive about their desire to celebrate and about the uncomfortable relationship not just to that imaginary past but to the painful present that goes with being a tourist from the overdeveloped world in the midst of African poverty.

BELL HOOKS It's interesting, too, to think about this in relation to the work you've been doing about the role that the remembrance of slavery plays in all of this. To really think about how even the incredible celebration of Toni Morrison's *Beloved* deals with these questions of memory. I found it interesting that somehow this fictive version of slavery was much more interesting to people than other ways of getting inside that history. You would have thought that there were no documents available to us in cheap paperback books that one could read and really learn about slavery. There was this sense that people really don't want to learn *that* sense of slavery. It's easier to read the narrative of slavery that's in *Beloved* than it is to actually read slave narratives. One doesn't necessarily lead into the other.

PAUL GILROY Are you saying that they point in different directions somehow? What are the consequences of that?

BELL HOOKS I think there are incredible passages in *Beloved* but I also think that slavery begins to have a kind of mythic quality there as well. Think about the scar on Sethe's body that has become like a tattoo almost, this fascinating representation. It's invoked almost as though it's a painting. That's very different from looking both at the economics of slavery and also the impact of slavery on contemporary black experience. We have very little work that tries to connect slavery to the periods that follow it. I would like there to be psycho-histories about the question of black people moving from the agrarian south to the industrialized north that wouldn't just be about naming that moment but about trying to look at the consequences of that shift for us today.

PAUL GILROY Do you know that wonderful passage towards the beginning of Walter Benjamin's essay 'The Storyteller'? Your last comments really brought it to mind. He was talking about the experiences of Europe after the 1914–18 war but for me there's something about the quality of his thoughts that makes them resonate strongly with the movement of black peoples into the modernity of the second industrial revolution. He writes: 'A generation that had gone to school on a horse-drawn street car now stood under the open sky in a countryside in which nothing remained unchanged but the clouds, and beneath these clouds, in a field of force of destructive torrents and explosions, was the tiny fragile human body.' In a way that doesn't fit us, but he points towards things that are useful. In him we can find, for example, a valuable refusal to buy into the whole idea of history as progress. This is connected to his Jewishness in some complex ways. There is also a dogged sense of the motion of history as inescapably catastrophic which resonates with themes in black vernacular culture. That idea of history as a ceaseless forward momentum produced by the engine of social and economic development – ever onward and upward – is another way in which contemporary Afrocentric thought is in thrall to and complicit with European assumptions and conventions. There is no sense that the concept of development might be problematic or that the ideology of progress itself might be something we should be cautious and sceptical about.

BELL HOOKS Don't you think that is a major critique that one could make of the black movements of political resistance in the United States from reconstruction on? Practically all forms of resistance took that model of progress and set it to work in the interests of black people. The buried history that isn't about that vision of progress is never invoked. Instead we have someone like Martin Delany who is totally locked into that idea of progress.

PAUL GILROY Yes, but I find it more excusable at that point in time than it is today. Then the arguments about literacy, education and citizenship as gauges of progress had an altogether different currency. People had just cast their shackles off. But in the light of what we have discovered since then about de-colonization, about the complex ways in which those struggles to enter the political process were repudiated, about the move into urban experience that you were describing earlier. Maybe those insights should prevent us from being too hasty in summoning the idea of progress into our discourse of legitimation.

BELL HOOKS One of the biggest differences between black experiences in the US and black experiences in Europe and elsewhere is that there hasn't been a major discourse on de-colonization in the US. Who would we cite in America on these questions? I have been looking at a lot of the new black nationalist writings to see if people have been reading Fanon and the others and they're not.

PAUL GILROY Is that because those writings are seen as tainted by Europe?

BELL HOOKS Absolutely, I think again there's a certain kind of political naivety around in black politics which means that words like 'colonization' and 'de-colonization' aren't allowed to play a role. Maybe that's why African Americans have to invent the wheel again and again and again around questions of self-esteem. I just feel very anguished that we should be still having discussions about issues like which dolls black children prefer to play with. 'Oh my God, they prefer white dolls!' That reproducing of the drama of victimization is totally tied to the lack of a whole critical theory and practice around colonization and de-colonization.

PAUL GILROY In the era of pan-African politics and in the 1960s there were attempts to make that connection. The notion of areas of black settlement in American cities as internal colonies appeared very spectacularly in the discourse of radical black politics for a while. What is it about the shift from a *pan*-Africanism to an *Afro*centrism that means this global dynamic gets lost? Does the very term 'pan-Africanism' allow for a sense of differences within blackness that Afrocentrism seems to want to conceal?

BELL HOOKS The myth of progress is part of this. It creates pressure to deny the patterns of victimization that don't make progress a simple matter either of material acquisition or of proving that we have the fruits provided by the knowledge that we created something spectacular in the past. I prefer a sense of progress that says 'what are the possibilities we can develop out of the present?' When we talk about transforming the lives of the black underclass in the US we really can't talk about significant changes that people foresee happening in the economy. There are other ways of understanding progress.

PAUL GILROY At that point you seem to be right on the edge of saying that we need to find a different way of talking about all this. The language of talking about it that foregrounds the concept of racism is now hostage to a sense of victimage that has some moral payoff and some psychological benefits but may not translate very effectively into the political sphere.

BELL HOOKS Well, that's why William Julius Wilson's book *The Declining Significance of Race* was so misunderstood. The title was very much undermining of the useful contribution of the book which was to say that we can no longer talk about black experience without a class analysis that is coordinated to the analysis of contemporary racism.

PAUL GILROY I take that point about Wilson's work. I think you are right, that was an important moment. Though the next stage in his thinking shows that questions of gender and power are impossible to grasp within the model of class politics to which he subscribes in *The Truly Disadvantaged*.

BELL HOOKS Absolutely, he takes us right away from naturalizing race but then gender gets to be what he naturalizes. That is where his conservative aspect comes out. It takes us right back to that patriarchal definition of progress. What must be done to heal the crisis of black Americans? You go back to a narrative of the family. It takes us back to the presence of a patriarch in the household as the thing which establishes whether progress has taken place.

PAUL GILROY Yesterday when we were looking at the Bloods and Crips plans for the rebuilding of LA I was struck by the richness and complexity of those proposals, by the absence of any Afrocentric tropes from those plans and thirdly, and this makes me very uncomfortable, by the incredible distance between that vision of social and economic reconstruction and the whole domain of African-American intellectual life which seems reluctant to turn its gaze towards those intractable conflicts.

BELL HOOKS Though the word 'de-colonization' isn't used in that plan, one can read it in that way. If we were to show it to certain thinkers in Third World countries they would recognize it in that way. How it talks about transforming the educational system, for example, its sense of a different approach to pedagogy. There have been very few black academics/intellectuals who have been interested in that area and its implications for rethinking public policy on schools. We can see that happening in the Bloods and Crips proposals for reconstructing LA.

PAUL GILROY When I read that plan I couldn't help thinking about South Africa and the whole project of social reconstruction and re-building of their educational system which is being engaged in there. The tasks that arise in reckoning with the existence of a whole generation of people who have been systematically excluded from those spaces. I wonder whether the experience of what has been happening there isn't a resource that we could use a lot more in making sense of some of the things around us in the other overdeveloped countries undergoing processes of de-industrialization. André Gorz, the French economist and philosopher, talks about the growth of types of service work here in Europe as being a process of South-Africanization. The return of household servants is one aspect of this that is relevant to what is going on here in London, the new politics of spatiality and zone-based control in our urban centres, the militarization of aspects of policing are other patterns that the South African experience can illuminate.

BELL HOOKS This takes us back once again to the necessity of not forgetting the history of slavery. So much of the South African economic system is similar to a slave system. Think about contemporary Africa on a global scale, there is so much that is being taken right back to a coercive unfree mode, bringing much of labour back to a slave-type situation where people are working eighteen or more hours each day to grow their coffee or some other commodity for the world market but are quite unable to feed themselves and their own communities. I think that people don't want to look at what this means. It isn't that familiar image of a Third-Worldness that doesn't want to work. What we see are people who never stop working incredible hours, whole families working but still not being able to eat. These are things that are hard for African Americans to face because they disrupt the myth of progress and say that there has to be some other type of strategy for a collective future that is not rooted in the type of materialism where we see the acquisition of goods and property as the principal sign of having made it. There is a lot of black academic work and representation of black intellectuals and academics themselves that suggests that this is how we still mea-sure our achievements.

PAUL GILROY What does it mean, then, when those same rather privileged intellectuals turn around and diagnose the experience of the black poor in the inner cities and denounce their choices and strategies for survival as 'nihilism'? In other words, when they argue that there is nothing constructive there that can be recovered and that life in the inner city is just a sort of culture of compensation, that is fratricidal and misogynistic and leads up a whole set of blind alleys politically. The other thing it makes me think is that you come from the south, from a rural background. What about the regional basis of these Afrocentric discourses and their concentration in particular locations? What would it mean to offer someone African identity and clothing and a new name in those parts of black America which are not urban and which are still part of an older 'peasant' experience that is much closer to slavery in its ways of organizing labour and relating to nature? What about the psycho-history of the people who didn't migrate northwards or drift into urban spaces? How different are they from those who did leave? Is Afrocentrism a form of nostalgia that thrives where that separation from the land and the scale of life associated with rural living are greatest? Something similar might be argued about the utterly different forms of Rastafari culture you find in the Jamaican countryside and, say, in inner London. If 'underclass' life is a culture of com-pensation, what is it compensation for?

BELL HOOKS That again takes us back to the question of

colonization. One of the important differences between an analysis based on colonization and one that can only speak in terms of race and racism is that, the moment you begin to talk about colonization, you *have* to place yourself globally. This means that the United States cannot stay at the centre of the analysis. You have to place issues of labour and class in a much more prominent place than many black scholars have wanted to place them. You also have to talk very, very differently about gender. One of the things that has been so saddening as I've gone around lecturing at different campuses this year is appreciating the force of a neo-black nationalism and Afrocentrism that denies gender as a problematic. It creates a fiction of our social reality that is so dangerous because it can't really see what's happening with black women. It can't see the fact that black women and children will constitute 75 per cent of the black poor in our midst in the near future. This situation makes the experience of being an African-American woman who's in the underclass much more similar to the situation of an African woman who is also part of an underclass. A great gulf is going to exist between those women and the experience of a black woman like myself whose position is very much in a bourgeois context. What I've been trying to argue in my lectures at the University of Utrecht is that there are going to be greater similarities between that under-class black woman in Africa somewhere in an urban context and the underclass black women in the United States. There will be more connections between those groups than with black people who have different class experiences. I think that's a social real-ity that black people in the US have tended to deny. In the rural south, farm land has been overworked and over-used. There's a kind of dispossession of black people in the agrarian parts of the US. Most of the Afrocentric thinking is coming from the urban parts of the country and they don't even deal with that. Who talks about the experience of black people in the south, people who still look to land and an agriculturally based economy for some sense of their well-being?

PAUL GILROY That may not even be a wholly capitalist set of social and economic arrangements. To talk about that southern experience would mean dealing with the survival within a capitalist structure of coercive production relations that belong to a pre-capitalist economic order.

BELL HOOKS One of the scary things that we can see is a similarity between so-called insurgent black intellectuals and more conservative intellectuals and academics. This is a growing refusal to critique capitalism or to offer any sense of a vision beyond it.

PAUL GILROY That's not just a problem for black intellectuals right now. There is an incredible squeamishness, particularly since the models of so-called actually existing socialism have been entirely discredited. We are being told pragmatically that some sort of liberal, redemptive incursion into the capitalist version of democratic political culture is the best thing that we can hope for. My response to that is to say that we need imaginative, utopian projections and aspirations more urgently than ever. That utopias aren't just a secret luxury we can quietly and discretely warm your hands around when the door is bolted and the curtains are drawn. We need to find a political language for projecting utopias out into the public domain. Maybe that is why Afrocentrism's myths of Africa are so powerful right now?

BELL HOOKS Absolutely. I find it fascinating that, when we look at the rise of certain young black male film-makers in the United States, people like Spike Lee and John Singleton, one of the things that they are very much embracing and preaching is a kind of myth of capitalism as working for you if you can simply find the right gimmick, produce your commodity and push. By saying that, I don't want to demean the notion of black businesses, but it's almost like sending a propagandistic message that capitalism is still working. In that fantastical Horatio Alger way: you just work hard enough and it will eventually pay off and you too can be a millionaire. It's a kind of rhetoric that denies a need for alternative visions. There's a kind of aggression in those representations of black reality that those film-makers make which suggests that any kind of suggestion that we need to envision utopia is portrayed as somehow non-black, as a non-black move.

PAUL GILROY Hasn't that got to do with the collapse of the authority of the Church as a complex of social institutions where that kind of necessary experimentation was mandated – 'I have been to the mountaintop' and so on?

BELL HOOKS I think that's very interesting because the Church wasn't just a place for conventional religiosity but a place for a transcendent vision of life that allowed for the formation of utopian discourses. One of the things that we ought to be asking is this. If we do away with the power of the Church, as has happened in black experience in the US, then what takes its place as something legitimizing the imagination of a future outside the existing social reality? Part of why so many African Americans are embracing an ideology of victimization (which I frankly see at the heart of a lot of Afrocentric thinking) is that we can only see ourselves as victims if we cannot get back to some glorified sense of our origins. To the degree that we collectively buy into that, there's a certain kind of doom. It feels to me like a very tragic moment in African-American history because of that sense that there are only two possibilities. You frame them in your work as the choice between identifying either with slaves or with pharaohs. Blac:ople used to identify with the slaves, the oppressed, andeve that there was some kind of redemptive model of resise that would create a transformed world where there wcbe access to material good or spiritual good available to evne. If there are only these two possibilities then we *must* iify with the pharoahs. There cannot be any possibility of se a resistance struggle that would lead us to a break with thanry opposition where we would be able to say that there are nole possibilities of social and political interaction that can pcowards resistance strategies that don't necessarily turn the vl into two groups: oppressors and oppressed.

PAUL GILROY Wve been very critical about some of the things that have been1g on in African-American political culture. But here we arèurope. You have been here for several weeks this time and I w you've been here before. What about the experience of b people and other minorities in Europe? Have your experiena Europe changed your understanding of the situation in Arra? Have you, for example, seen anything here that has helped to develop your understanding of what the politics of race.der and class might mean back home?

BELL HOOKS It'sly interesting that, in coming back to London and comparing1th the situation in the Netherlands, I get the feeling that blaeople there aren't really dealing with the complexity of theirory or their location within colonialism in a way that is carable to what is going on here. In London there seems to lch a great population of black peoples, South Asians, Africararibbeans, who are able to engage in different ways with the cions of colonialism and de-colonization. One of the reasons many of us in the States have become interested in Europreared black thinkers is that we are in need of the kind of ans that people are able to produce here, readings that allow for more complex renderings of black experience globally.

PAUL GILROY If you look back to the early years of this century, you do find those global links being made from within black American political culture. It's odd that there seem to be times when making these links in the political imagination is possible and other periods in which it becomes much more difficult. Du Bois provides the most obvious example of someone trying to make those connections meaningfully, to show that the problem of white supremacy has a global significance, to explore the possibility of anti-imperialist political alliances and to take black Americans beyond what sometimes looks like a rather parochial inventory of political concerns. Why do these initiatives get literally written out of the version of the history of black American political culture that gets the stamp of orthodoxy?

BELL HOOKS That has a lot to do with the assimilation of black academics to white institutions. There was such a strong sense in the early twentieth century that black people who were deeply intellectual had to turn to other countries apart from the US to get validation of their place as intellectuals. Someone like Du Bois was much more affirmed outside the US as an intellectual. The way that black people evoke him today is not the way that he was evoked. There is a sense that they had to get beyond the boundaries of nationality in order to discover dimensions of the self it was impossible to discover while remaining in the United States. I was saying to Isaac Julien that we don't have a space yet in black cultural production in the US for people to produce work like *Looking for Langston* or *Testament* because there's still this insistence on a simplistic visualization of black experience. I think, again, that's why there's a greater bonding than ever before between black cultural workers in the US and

Britain. We're grasping at other versions of black culture and politics in order to go forward in our work. This puts us at odds with the place of black thinkers in the traditional academy. I don't think that academy has ever been rewarding of progressive black intellectual thought: de-colonized thought. The great thinkers of de-colonization, including Du Bois, had to move out of the white university *and* the black university as well. It's interesting to think about the enormous economic power that certain select groups of black people have in the US yet we still don't have a number of institutes that could look at black experience outside of a predominantly conservative, white institutional framework. That says a lot to me. Why don't these things exist? Look at the state of black publishing too. What we see there is an incredible loss.

PAUL GILROY That's true, but what you also have is a flow of black popular culture that is an incredible global resource.

BELL HOOKS We see a return to that area now. It's not unlike the Harlem Renaissance period. All of a sudden the black bourgeoisie, including the academics, are trying to appropriate the radical potentiality that lies within that popular culture by producing a layer of critical thinking that attempts to oversee that popular culture. I think, for example, of Henry Louis Gates Jnr's involvement in the 2 Live Crew case. He hasn't identified himself with the progressive strands of rap but then comes in as a kind of expert player who identifies which forms of black popular culture can be seen as connected to black history. Rather than connecting Public Enemy to a history of resistance, we have a black intellectual defining for us that 2 Live Crew represent a continuum of black traditions of signifying. We all had the experience of going to the black popular culture conference organized at the DIA Foundation. Why did that happen now? Many of those people – important black academics – have not shown an interest in popular culture. Why should they develop it at this particular moment? What they are doing acts to police black popular culture and to ferret out those aspects of that popular culture that are very transgressive. There's a masking of a lot of the radical potential in black popular culture.

PAUL GILROY What struck me about that event was how little of what was actually said engaged with popular culture at all. I am more optimistic than you about the capacity of that culture to resist the policing gestures that are undoubtedly there.

BELL HOOKS Part of why you can be more optimistic is that often that aspect of black popular culture that carries over to Europe is that which is most interesting and challenging. Those forms, because of the conservatism of mass media in the United States, are the ones that get most obscured at home. However one sees the Disposable Heroes of Hip-hoprisy, I have seen them get more press and television exposure here and in the Netherlands than in the US. Any black rap group that is focusing on the normal materialist misogynistic stuff is going to get enormous play back home.

PAUL GILROY The popularity of materialism and misogyny is partly a result of the fact that those images of blackness are the mechanisms of the 'cross-over' relationship. They are in a sense the most comfortable representations of blackness. They are the images that the dominant culture finds easiest to accept, process and take pleasure in. So often the medium for their transmission is a discourse on black masculinity that constructs black men as both sources of pleasure and sources of danger to white listeners and spectators. Some black cultural producers accept these images and have tried collusively or instrumentally to exploit them, both in their strategies for cross-over sales and in meeting the expectations of a black public that has internalized them as definitions of what blackness is now about.

BELL HOOKS The importance of those images is that they disrupt essentialist representations of blackness. It's interesting that we can have that strand in black popular culture. In a lot of black critical thought there's a real strong attempt right now to recoup an essentialist identity politics. Often it demands the verification and valorization of those same images. It doesn't want to talk about any sense of cross-over that isn't rooted in a sense of betrayal. I think that's been very hard for black people globally. I have been seeing that both in Europe and in the US. The problem gets made worse in the absence of theorics of black experience that could allow us not just to superficially name the complexities of black popular culture but to openly say what we might gain from using the white Euro-based theory that many of us read and find challenging. I would like to connect the black conservative movement in the academy that I have described with the work of someone like Camille Paglia. Part of her repudiation of European theory can be tied to the anti-intellectualism in black culture right now. The same repudiation is also taking place in an essay like Barbara Christian's 'The Race for Theory'. It seems to me that sort of thinking can have so much more force among blacks precisely because we have so little writing that speaks to the need to use diverse materials to make better theoretical sense of our histories and contemporary experiences. That is very frightening because, despite the growth of interest in cultural studies, there is very little new thinking being done about how one theorizes black experience and *how* one theorizes the black popular. One thing about the black popular culture conference was that it was often the young voices, the ones that were closest to the spaces of black cultural production, that were the least interesting in what they had to say about the culture. That was very frightening.

PAUL GILROY I don't disagree with that. We know we have to enter those spaces and to fight within them for politically engaged and informed critical practice but we should also appreciate that people can be very easily distracted, even bought off, by the glamour and the money, the power and pleasures offered by the capital-intensive institutions of cultural production. There are questions of political generation too. In England, many of the younger people in black cultural production haven't had any exposure to radical political movements at all. Their political essentialism often fits neatly with their entrepreneurial aspirations. They are sceptical of the left and may also find the twists and turns of organized sexual politics hard to follow when its insights look to them like good sense. Among those who oppose essentialism, post-modernism has licensed a kind of playfulness that can trivialize the political stakes and minimize the difficulties of actually changing anything institutional.

BELL HOOKS I have been thinking about the institutionalization of feminist theory-making and thinking in the US Academy. If you go to a feminist conference you won't see different models of critical debate and discussion being created. It'll be the same old model of standing up, giving your paper and then having questions and answers. All of us are having to look and ask whether this type of model ever really subverted or even altered dominant models of intellectual dialogue. We have to deal with the absence in the US of spaces for critical discussion and debate. It was at the black popular culture conference that I first heard you publicly pushing your critique of the idea of home, the evocation of home, in black political culture as a special place – the founding site of resistance. Many black Americans responded very negatively to that but the structure didn't allow for any discussion of what you were saying. We couldn't work through that difference.

PAUL GILROY One of the places where we can push each other to be more imaginative about images we can use in the future is around the idea of kinship. I see black political culture as being host to very different and contested ideas about what kinship is and how it works. There's one language for this that comes out of the Church: brother and sister. This is a democratic and antiphonal one but can also be quite authoritarian in some of its characteristics. For a long period that political language struggled against a very patriarchal alternative that stressed the centrality and significance of male heads of household and was tied into the bitter policy questions about the reconstruction and revalorization of the black family. Now that these issues have been taken over into discussion of the urban underclass in American cities and your political and economic crises are being so powerfully represented as a crisis of black masculinity, the inclination to run back to that discourse of the familial and find shelter there, particularly when the democratic alternative has been weakened by the Church's own loss of power, is a big problem.

BELL HOOKS Work like mine that really tried to talk about the rearticulation of the politics of home, using elements of the same framework, has been really undermined. There hasn't been a body of black women and men thinkers around gender that have created enough of a different discourse on home and family that can challenge the earlier codes. I can tell you when you challenge me that I am not thinking about that patriarchal model but it's clear that my thinking isn't making any kind of major intervention in how black people are looking back to the family.

Someone like Patricia Hill Collins, for example, in *Black Feminist Thought*, is still very rooted in conservative and traditional notions of home and family. Her work can be evoked to say 'here's a black feminist analysis' but it's one that doesn't challenge that construction of family and home at all.

PAUL GILROY In her work and in the work of others too, that sentimental and authoritarian construction of family, home and community is the site of a break from the dreaded 'white feminism'. In a way, that's what makes it especially attractive to some people who use it as a cipher for their own sense of what a feminist politics is about to become.

BELL HOOKS Yes, I think we've talked a lot in the past about how white women can become comfortable with that because they can be happy with the image of the separatist black woman who isn't trying to bring any sort of critical reading to feminist theory in general and who says 'the only sort of discourse that interests me is the one around race and racism'.

PAUL GILROY And who orients that politics through experiences of victimage and recovery which take place emphatically in the private sphere.

BELL HOOKS I think that is something that makes it hard for us to create a group of dissident, insurgent black intellectuals who are moving in new ways on a different ground. Those young thinkers don't get affirmed. Often students are searching for that affirmation and leaving those schools where an essentialist understanding around Afrocentrism predominates and trying to locate spaces where they can develop different kinds of work. Manning Marable was saying jokingly at a conference he had the other day that what we need are progressive multiculturally based institutions. We talked about the question of money. Where would we ever get the funding base that could make that happen? Perhaps we have to go back to nineteenth-century models. If Mary McLeod Bethune had been thinking 'I need a grant from the Rockefeller foundation before I can do anything', what would have happened? We have to get back to the idea that there can be little school houses, little spaces of learning that won't necessarily have lots of resources.

PAUL GILROY I have been criticized a lot here, by Kobena Mercer in particular, for my attempts to argue for an anti-state orientation in the area of black cultural politics. This is seen as an economistic and leftist residue. The Gramscian analysis of power and politics can be blended with cynicism and corruption. It can be made to say that we should get into the powerful, big and rich institutions and fight the famous war of position there. We should open up the internal cracks, find the fissures. We can be inside and against. We get inside the TV. We get inside the arts bodies. We get inside the multinationals. This too can license an anything-goes attitude which is basically individualistic. Sometimes, inside and against isn't going to be habitable or even possible. The 'against' part gets readily forgotten when the cheques are signed. There are limits to how the weak can exploit the strong. There's a price we pay for getting into some of those spaces.

BELL HOOKS You use the construction inside and against. In the US we have worked out the inside but what is not worked out is the against. The against is where we must also be outside those places using time and resources to create different possibilities. But there has been a complete failure to do this. One would think that we could go to many cities in the US and find alternative community spaces that coexist with the overground ones.

We just don't have those spaces right now. It's scary that they are not happening. If we are only seeing the established educational institutions as the location of education for critical consciousness, we become complicit in widening a gap. Let's face it, a lot of black thinkers in the past came out of the underclass. Now most black folks who come into educational institutions are coming from privileged material locations. We no longer have structures that allow for the fact that a lot of brilliant, gifted black children and people reside in the underclass and need to have paths that allow them to cross boundaries and find opportunities. People have been turning their backs on that constituency. I think people haven't been willing to hear that kind of critique of institutions or ask why this is happening. There could be a bell hooks because there were those kind of black community institutions. The church as I experienced it was an alternative site for education, for critical consciousness. The black books that weren't in the white school I went to were in the church library. Even in my own home church, the library doesn't seem to have the place in the imagination of the Church that it had then.

PAUL GILROY That's really interesting to me. I have been thinking a lot recently about the way that the culture of the image is working so powerfully now to exacerbate some of the divisions and differences within black communities and to work against the historic authority of popular cultural forms based around music and print and around rituals in the public sphere, not just the worship but profane public rituals too.

BELL HOOKS There was a recognition that black people could produce culture if it had meaning and value, even if it did not sell. Now, nothing that doesn't sell, that doesn't provide an immediate gain, can have value. That's a way of thinking that undermines the possibility of black creativity. It commodifies, it says don't waste your time creating anything that you are not going to be able to make money out of.

PAUL GILROY Yes, think about the difference between taking a musician, singer or preacher as your archetypal model of black creativity and taking a film-maker in Hollywood today as the image that supplies the logic and the inspiration to your creative hopes.

BELL HOOKS In your study, I was looking at the new book by Bob O'Meally about Billie Holiday. On one hand, we see those forms of victimization that defined her life. On the other, we see that this person wasn't sitting around thinking of what song she's going to create that was going to give her the greatest amount of cross-over return. Part of why we'll be in danger if we don't create an analysis of black cultural production that includes class is that we can overlook how black people have internalized a First-World Western materialism that governs our strategies for information sharing and knowledge production.

PAUL GILROY What role do transnational and intercultural dimensions play in restoring vitality to a black public world where identities and political subjectivities are made and remade and where differences can be negotiated against some background of affinity – a global communitarian moment?

BELL HOOKS One thing that comes to mind is that the black underclass of the US would have to see their situation in a relative way. If, for example, you think about water use globally, those people who may be unemployed in the United States but who still have constant access to water by turning a tap, or light available by just turning a switch, are in a relative position of power over basic resources in daily life that the masses of people don't have. Here's another thing that has been frightening. Growing up poor in the south, our parents still said 'think of the starving': in other words think about what you mean when you invoke deprivation and scarcity in relation to a global context. These ideas seemed so annoying then but they make a lot of sense to me now.

PAUL GILROY Wasn't the Church a conduit for that global sensibility too?

BELL HOOKS Absolutely, because of the whole missionary thing. Ironically that is what Alice Walker recoups in *The Color Purple* though I didn't find the way she did it all that interesting. The fact is that there was a realistic sense of Africa that was rooted in the missionary movement. However corrupt and culturally biased that movement was, it did create a sense that black people in the US did not exist on an island where we were measuring ourselves against the white ruling class to see whether we've made it or not. You're placing yourself in a global context. In the US right now we aren't growing in our recognition of that. We are actually trying to repress the recognition of that awareness. I'd like to end by highlighting some of where I think a sense of hope lies. One important thing for me is making a space of dialogue and collaborative work.

PAUL GILROY Yes. It's been really important to me that we've been able to have such a wide-ranging conversation. A dialogue like this is special, not because it represents the quest for consensus but because it shows that in disagreeing with each other we can provide the basis for a sense of community.

16 Wearing your art on your sleeve

Notes towards a diaspora history of black ephemera

*As perhaps the first of the technological artistic inventions, it
[the phonograph record] already stems from an era that
cynically acknowledges the dominance of things over people
through the emancipation of technology from human
requirements and human needs and through the presentation
of achievements whose significance is not primarily humane;
instead, the need is initially produced by advertisement, once
the thing already exists and is spinning in its own orbit.*

T. W. Adorno

*While we were in Lagos we visited Fela Ransome Kuti's club
the Afro Spot, to hear him and his band. He'd come to hear
us, and we came to hear him. I think when he started as a
musician he was playing a kind of music they call Highlife,
but by this time he was developing Afro-beat out of African
music and funk. He was kind of like the African James
Brown. His band had strong rhythm . . . Some of the ideas
my band was getting from that band had come from me in
the first place, but that was okay with me. It made the music
that much stronger.*

James Brown

Special cultural and political relationships have been
created in the Atlantic 'triangle' of the African diaspora. They

are the outcome of long processes in which the cultures of Africa, the Americas, Europe and the Caribbean have interacted and transformed each other. Their complex history cannot be presented in detail here[1] but it has involved struggles that dissolve the separation between politics and cultural expression. They have been concerned with the abolition of slavery and the acquisition of political rights for black Americans, the independence of colonial countries and the solidarity of diaspora blacks with movements for the destruction of racist settler regimes in Africa. These struggles are notable for the way they have been infused with the spiritual rhetoric and messianic visions of the black Church. They have involved the movement of key individuals, the international circulation of books, tracts and pamphlets and, perhaps above all, they have been signalled through the transnational power of black musics which have reached out beyond the boundaries of the nation-state. These struggles have also relied on the circulation of images and symbols.

Against this background, I want to explore one means through which cultural and aesthetic exchanges between different populations across the diaspora have been constructed – one population providing cultural and philosophical fuel for another and vice versa. It may, at first sight, appear to be trivial and inconsequential to focus on gramophone records as a medium through which these diasporic conversations have been conducted, particularly as they are commodities that are designed to be ephemeral, giving way to replacements once boredom has set in or fashions have changed. Black music has, however, only partially obeyed the ground rules of reification and planned obsolescence. Its users have sometimes managed to combine the strongest possible sense of fashion with a respectful, even reverent approach to the historical status of their musical culture which values its longevity and its capacity to connect them to their historical roots. The music has thus often been prized more for its sublimity and the racial probity of its witness to their lives than for its precarious status as a disposable and replaceable fragment of pop culture.

I will not, however, examine records solely for the music that they contain. They should be understood as complex cultural artefacts – objects – in their own right. The music recorded and encoded onto the surface of the discs may be the primary inducement to acquire a record, but the sleeve with its combination of text and images comprises an important, if secondary, element that so far seems to have escaped sustained consideration from cultural historians of black experience.

The rise of the long-playing, 33 rpm, vinyl gramophone record coincides neatly with turbulent years of black struggle in the United States and it provides a valuable means to examine both that history and its international impact. The corporate replacement of LP records by cassettes, CDs and other new digital formats is having profound and dismal consequences for the circulation and use of black music. CDs do their work in secret, shut away from the disruptive, creative power of black hands once that mysterious drawer is closed. But it is not only that the specific forms of vernacular creativity constituted around vinyl discs cannot be maintained in the newer formats. Reissues of back catalogue are selective and completely out of step with the needs of the black underground, let alone the demands of cultural history. This means that some of the most dynamic traffic in our cultural heritage comes to an abrupt halt as more and more records simply cannot be replaced. We are left with different kinds of commodity which are experienced and used differently. Images and text have been shrunk. Both the ratio between them and their relationship to the music have been transformed.

 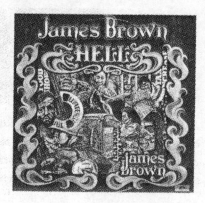

The text and images found on sleeves existed in relation to the music they enclosed but these different dimensions of communication had a significant measure of independence from each other. Together they constituted an intricate commodity that fused different components of black cultural and political sensibility in an unstable and unpredictable combination. In the 1960s and 1970s, black political discourse migrated to and colonized the record sleeve as a means towards its expansion and self-development. That era is now over.

I have argued elsewhere[2] that the social relations that surround the consumption of African diaspora musics and the forms that these musics assume, do not fit easily into the saleable segments that their status as cultural commodities requires. The history of black musical forms includes a constant struggle

against both the constraints of the technology of musical reproduction and dominant expectations of how music, packaged and
sold in this way, should be heard. The imagery on record sleeves
was a minor, though still significant, part of this struggle. Those
who provide the means that can translate the substance of black
creativity into two ounces of plastic with a hole in the middle,
wrap it in paper, cardboard and plastic, and then ship it around
the world in order to maximize their profit, have been unable to
command this convoluted distributive process in its entirety. The
musicians who created the music did not always control its packaging, but they were sometimes able to use cover art to collude
with their preferred audiences in telling ways which the multinational companies who circulated these products either did not
care about or were unable to foresee. For example, the preva-
lence of images of ancient Egypt during the 1960s and 1970s
proved to be an important means for communicating pan-
African ideas in an inferential, populist manner. It is worth noting that, appropriated in this way, the 'traditional' imagery of
ancient Egypt was not counterposed to views of 'modern' reality
but rather presented in a way that emphasized its continuity with
contemporary technological and scientific developments.

It is noteworthy that, although these images are still part of the visual culture that supports African-American music, they were used in a number of rather different ways during the 1980s. One recent version mediates the heritage of Nile Valley civilizations by inserting the borrowed and 'blackened' image of Indiana Jones, the superhuman hero from Steven Spielberg's adventure films, between the cartouche and the viewer.

African-American music has frequently been sent out into the world in open, 'provisional' formats which anticipate the supplementary work that active consumers must bring to the ritual settings in which it will be played, if it is to reveal its full power.

This argument can be extended beyond the specifically musical dimensions of the record as a cultural commodity. Parallel and essentially similar processes of aesthetic and political grounding can be shown to be at work in the invitation to 'read' and make active use of images and text on record sleeves. In order to appreciate the significance of the imagery of race that record sleeves project, it is essential to remember that we are dealing with a dispossessed and economically exploited population which does not enjoy extensive opportunities to perceive itself or see its experiences imaginatively or artistically reflected in the visual culture of urban living. As far as Britain is concerned, blacks have been seldom seen in advertisements or on television. The pictorial symbols inherent in the political agitation of their communities, in independently published magazines or the minority markets in specialized items like cosmetics which have displayed the cultural assets and distinctiveness of the 'racial' group, are limited and meagre visual resources by comparison with the mainstream media. The cultural significance of record covers as a form of folk art is therefore enhanced simply because they offer one of very few opportunities to see and enjoy images of black people outside the stereotyped guises in which the dominant culture normally sanctions their presence. For example, this simple family snapshot of the Marleys would never have emerged while his record company was promoting him as a swaggering and sexually available Rastaman shrouded by a cloud of ganga smoke. This variety of hyper-masculine representation had been thought essential to the development of Marley's appeal to rock audiences. This picture only appeared as a curiosity in the nostalgic moment after his death in 1981.

Showing something of how the record sleeve fits into vernacular cultural and political history is relatively easy in black America. There, the depth and vitality of musical traditions means that the recent history of black life has been registered in the most minute detail through the imagery found on disc sleeves, the titles of the records and their changing appeals to different groups of black and white consumers. The formation and transcendence of the market for 'race records' is there to behold. The secularization of black music which led to soul, the civil rights struggles and, in particular, the Black Power movement, can all be apprehended by this means. The ebbs and flows in black political culture have been faithfully transcribed through the text, imagery and artwork of the record sleeve.

This story is made more complex by questions of musical genre[3] and of course, by the shifting relationship between independent black record production and the multinational companies that dominate the music industries. Marketing jazz is necessarily different from marketing soul, hip-hop, house or reggae. Each sub-category creates its own rules, styles and strategies of visual communication which require detailed consideration. However, some tentative generalizations can be made. On the most basic level, sleeves have been used to define artists and to assist in the process of locating them into the particular area of the market to which they have been assigned by the record company, but this has not been their sole function. Apart from their use as a means to tell an audience how to hear and comprehend the music they enclose, sleeves have been developed as an agitational or educational tool which can, for example, encourage people to register to vote, to grow their hair a certain way, to wear a particular garment or to employ a familiar item of clothing in an unfamiliar and 'sub-culturally' distinctive way. Album jackets may also convey useful information to a specially targeted audience which is not the same as the one in which the record company is interested. They may also help to solicit this audience into specific modes of cultural and political identification. Most importantly for my purposes here, record sleeves have been employed to address the black public and to induce that public to assess and possibly to share in the styles and symbols that constitute the idea of blackness itself. The music facilitates the circulation of styles and symbols, creating an aura of pleasure and desire around them which is an important political phenomenon. This process has not always been a simple extension of the sale of records.

These developments may have been most obvious during the 1960s when the presentation of the black body had a crucial symbolic significance in the ideology of Black Power and its cultural correlates. However, the recent controversy over the cosmetic surgical operations undertaken by performers like Michael Jackson and George Benson shows that these issues are still politically charged and articulated into a broader network of American racial politics.[4] Arguments over surgical 'Europeanization' also apply to the lesser but more widespread practice of photographical whitening which has been a notable feature of the marketing of rhythm-and-blues artists as pop singers to white audiences during the 1980s.

The sheer intensity of feeling generated by these issues needs to be explained. It derives not simply from the belief that these ploys place the racial identity of black artists in jeopardy. It stems from the special conception of responsibility allocated to the artist in black expressive culture whereby musicians are seen as a priestly caste charged (among other things) with the custodianship of the racial group's most intimate self-identity. The black body, publicly displayed by the performer, becomes a privileged 'racial' sign. It makes explicit the hidden links between blacks and helps to ground an oppositional aesthetic constituted around our phenotypical difference from 'white' ideals of beauty and a concept of the body in motion which is the residue of our African cultures. When Prince, whose faithful adherence to the performative and aesthetic strategies of black America is thought by some commentators to contrast sharply with his calculated androgyny,[5] declares himself to be the son of a white woman in the 'autobiographical' film *Purple Rain*, a further layer of difficulty begins to take shape. This cover was produced prior to his marketing to whites as a rock artist.

Hair has provided the primary means to express these aesthetic and stylistic concerns[6] but the public display of Afrocentric *styles* – of dress, language and social conduct – remains a major consideration for both men and women. Long before the mass marketing of recorded music, black musicians, sacred and profane, had a special role in signifying black style in general and coolness[7] in particular to the black publics constituted in the dynamic act of performance. Ralph Ellison put it like this in 1964:

> Bessie Smith might have been a 'blues queen' to the society at large, but within the tighter Negro community where the blues was part of a total way of life, and a major expression of an attitude toward life, she was a priestess, a celebrant who affirmed the values of the group and man's ability to deal with chaos.[8]

These images of Aretha Franklin, presented, fifteen years apart, on the covers of her two double albums of religious music, actualize this role in strikingly different ways that convey much of how black America changed between 1972 and 1987. The African costume on the earlier sleeve is only the most obvious clue to the different notions of femininity that are being invoked. In the first picture she waits outside the church, possibly for baptism. In the second she is inside, her garments of heavenly white convey the fact that she has now been saved. These changes can be explained, not simply by the fact that Aretha has aged, but by the way that the Jackson presidential candidacy, which took black politics to a new position within the official political culture, recomposed the relationship between sacred and secular elements of black cultural struggle. If the church building represents America, what are we to make of Aretha's entry? The later record included a lengthy oration by Jackson himself. With Aretha's help, he was able to address her audience directly rather than rely on her art to transpose his message, 'I know it's dark but the morning had to come', into another *musical* discourse.

These pictures of Aretha are also a means to emphasize that men and women may encounter these images of blackness in different ways and put them to different kinds of use. Blackness appears in gender-specific forms that allow for the construction of distinctive modes of masculinity and femininity which, though connected by a common 'racial' identity, may be actively antagonistic. Sometimes the mode of this antagonism is taken to represent an internal truth of the black condition. Particularly in rhythm and blues, ritual conflict between men and women is dramatized so that it becomes a heavily encoded symbol of racial difference and racial distinctiveness. Some covers realize this visually, signifying blackness through the special intensity at which, it is believed, both gender difference and the conflict between men and women can be experienced.

The black population of Britain has a unique place within these complicated discursive relationships. Although there have been substantial black populations in Britain for a considerable period of time, the bulk of contemporary settlement is a post-war phenomenon. This means that the black British are a comparatively new and fragmented population. Black Britain has been heavily reliant on the output of black populations elsewhere for the raw materials from which its own distinctive, cultural and political identities could be assembled. The proximity of Britain's black settlers to the experience of migration also means that the cultures of the Caribbean have provided important resources which enabled people to retain and re-create links with the cultures from which they came. This has not, however, been a one-way street.

The different varieties of visual imagery used to sell Jimi Hendrix's music on the different sides of the Atlantic can be cited as an example here. In Britain Hendrix, a black American, was sold in conjunction with images of exoticism and transgression. In Britain, for example, his portrait was banished to the interior of the 'Electric Ladyland' sleeve by David King's celebrated photograph of nineteen naked women. Eighteen of them are 'white'; a lone black woman sits vacantly in the right mid-ground, offering a striking image of Hendrix's own displacement and isolation.

The cover of his second album release, 'Axis Bold As Love' went so far as to offer a painting of him in the guise of a Hindu deity. On the other side of the ocean, he was projected as a flower child produced from the womb of swinging London rather than a veteran rhythm-and-blues player. Indeed, his pedigree in the traditions of black music-making was perceived as an active hindrance to his serious status as a successful rock artist.[9] Finding two competent white sidemen who could also back-comb their hair into an approximation of his grown-out process-cum-proto 'fro style, became a means to undermine any lingering residues of blackness. Hendrix is an important, if exceptional, case because in neither place was he primarily marketed to a black audience.

The diasporic relationship between American and Caribbean cultures is also an increasingly complicated one. It is made yet more so by the cross-fertilization of musical styles that has followed the relocation of Caribbean people in the US, particularly in New York.[10] It is essential to remember that reggae is itself a composite, hybrid form which derives in part from jazz, rhythm and blues and soul styles. The cultures of black America have also supplied a political language to the world-wide black public. First the rhetoric of rights and justice, then the discourse of Black Power crossed the seas and enabled black folks here, there and everywhere to make sense of the segregation, oppression and exploitation they experienced in their countries of residence. With this in mind, it is perhaps unsurprising that the style of reggae culture in its reggae and its raggamuffin phases has been imported into the mainstream of black America through the visual culture of hip-hop.

The meaning of these imported cultural forms was not fixed or finally established at their point of origin, and it bears repetition that they too were offered outwards to the wider black world in radically unfinished forms that anticipated, even expected, supplementary input and further developmental work. In the cultural and aesthetic histories of diaspora populations, this anticipation of supplementation applies as readily to the visual meanings through which blackness is articulated as it does to its textual, verbal and performative figurations. The secret codes of black style and fashion have operated as a silent anti-language that connected us to each other in spite of wide variations in culture and lived experience.

In the past, I described the role of music in constituting an

alternative public sphere in which the self-understanding of particular black populations has been negotiated. The public institutions in which the music is actively and socially consumed are
an essential part of this process but they do not exhaust it. My
previous discussion of these issues centred on the affirmative
potency of the dancehall and the medley of social and cultural
practices – dance, word play, scratching, dubbing and mixing –
that are assembled and rearticulated there. To conclude, I want
to take this argument back one step by looking at the black
record shop as a similar kind of cultural institution, distinguished from the dancehall by the way that the music is complemented there by a proliferation of *visual* signs of blackness.

Like the barbershop, the record shop was a special social
place. In Britain, where 'front lines' exist without ghetto communities comparable with those of America or the Caribbean,
the role of the record shop as a popular cultural archive and
repository of folk knowledge is especially significant. It stores
some of the key cultural resources of the racial group and provides an autonomous space in which the music, language and
style that enable people to bring meaning and order to their
social lives can be worked out and worked on. Unlike America,
black Britain also lacked any significant opportunities for the
radio play of black music until the pirate radio movement of the
1980s. Without radio, record shops and clubs had an additional
significance in that they were the principal places where music,
denied overground exposure, could be heard. They provided
centres for its dissemination within the cultural underground
and constituted the pathways through which communities of
sentiment and interpretation could develop. I am suggesting,
then, that the untidy 'patchwork' effect of record sleeves on the
walls of these shops contributes substantially to the grounded,
profane aesthetics of Britain's black cultural idiom. How the
images are grouped together – whether, for example, styles like

reggae, soul or hip-hop appear together or are separated – become significant issues. The pressure of space is itself a factor in this. The shops are often extraordinarily small[11] and the lack of any browsing or rack space for displaying the product means that the walls take on an enhanced function in revealing what is on sale and in providing an ever-changing and seemingly organic agglomeration of covers, posters and advertisements which complement the power of sound with a montage of vernacular visual codes.

The urban location of the record shop, like the urban connotations of the music itself, are also a powerful means to draw together the discrepant sensibilities of scattered black populations. A sense of the city as a place where racial particularity grows into unique patterns is something central to the tradition of music-making which culminated in rhythm and blues. It comes across strongly in three strikingly different images from each of the preceding decades. All of them use the same urban environment to make their statements but in dissimilar ways.

The first shows The Impressions, photographed amidst the rubble of Chicago's South Side. The acoustic guitar that Curtis Mayfield clutches is an emblem of the trio's historical rootedness. They are an absolutely 'natural' presence in this landscape.

It is their territory the viewer is asked whether the title of the record refers to thetto in which we see them or to America as a whole. The banuld have just emerged from a cellar, prepared to make tlbeautiful music in what remains of the street. The presencan instrument also emphasizes the decline of images of perfance in contemporary packaging. The second picture, from mid-1970s shows George Clinton and his spaceship. Is he ang or departing? I have argued before that images like this ex; a utopian desire to escape from the order of racial oppressics well as a cosmic pessimism that despairs over the possibilit actual flight. In Clinton's hands, the hi-tech imagery of inlanetary travel is tamed by its association with the ancient wm of African civilizations. Clinton's image has been superimpl on his ghetto environment – the organic link which tied Cito it has been broken. The picture works through the contibetween the spaceship and its downbeat context, and this ion is repeated in the gulf that appears to separate the musicm the social location in which the listener

is likely to encou it. The third picture comes from Alyson Williams's 1989 an 'Raw'. This cover is clearly the product of a period whercord companies gained a much greater degree of corporantrol over the image-making process and where the importance of video, particularly for artists who might sell to white audiences, demands a close coordination of cover art with television imagery. Alyson is, significantly, a much a larger presence in the sleeve photograph than either of the other artists. Although her image has, like Clinton's, been super-imposed, it is somehow much more closely tied to its artificial background. She may have walked up the alley on her way to a party or a modelling assignment. However, the street is once again being used to convey something fundamental about the nature of the music itself. The combination of decay and sophis-tication in the image convey the blend of upmarket soul and homegirl hip-hop that characterizes her music. The radical implications of the picture become clearer if we set it alongside some images taken from competing black pop releases by female singers from the same period. Unlike Alyson, who is assertively at home in the street, Karyn White is happier and most fully her-self in the private sphere. She was photographed, apparently in the throes of pre-coital rapture, by an unmade bed. Vanessa Williams is pictured without any background at all, her notori-ety as a disgraced Miss America being all the prospective pur-chaser of her record needed to put it in the right context.

The continuity of the street as a backdrop for these three covers is much more significant than their obvious differences. It offers a valuable glimpse of the structure of feeling that underlies the political culture to which these images contribute and of which they are part.

'Consumption' is a vague word that trips far too easily off the dismissive tongue. People *use* these images and the music that they enclose for a variety of reasons. For the black user of these images and products, multivariant processes of 'consumption' may express the need to belong, the desire to make the beauty of blackness intelligible and somehow to fix that beauty and the pleasures it creates so that they achieve, if not permanence, then at least a longevity that retrieves them from the world of pop ephemera and racial dispossession. However trivial the black music record sleeve may seem to the outsider, it points to a fund of aesthetic and philosophical folk knowledge which the record as a commodity has been made to contain *in addition* to its reified pleasures. The presence of this extra cultural resource does not, of course, negate or deny the act of capitalistic exchange through which the record is usually acquired. But the guidance, solace and pleasures which that commodity may impart cannot be understood as an incidental adjunct to the sometimes solitary act of purchasing it.

Notes

1. Joseph Harris, *Global Dimensions of the African Diaspora*, Howard University Press, Washington D.C., 1982. Martin Kilson and Robert Rotberg (eds), *The African Diaspora: Interpretive Essays*, Harvard University Press, 1976.
2. *There Ain't No Black in the Union Jack*, Hutchinson, London, 1987.
3. Herman Gray, *Producing Jazz: The Experience of an Independent Record Company*, Temple University Press, Philadelphia, 1988.

4. Nelson George, *The Death of Rhythm and Blues*, Omnibus Press, London, 1988.

5. Ibid. Amiri Baraka, 'Class Struggle in Music', *The Black Nation*, vol. 5, no 1, Summer/Fall 1986.

6. Kobena Mercer, 'Black Hair Style Politics', *New Formations*, no. 3, 1987.

7. Robert Farris Thompson, 'An Aesthetic of the Cool: West African Dance', *African Forum*, vol. 2, pt 2, Fall 1966.

8. *Shadow and Act*, Random House, New York, 1964, p. 157.

9. Charles Shaar Murray, *Crosstown Traffic*, Faber, London, 1989.

10. Steven Hager, 'Africa Bambaataa's Hip Hop', *Village Voice*, 21 September 1982.

11. Dub Vendor in Ladbroke Grove, Footprintz, Quaff and Light and Sound in Finsbury Park or Don Christie's original shop in the Ladypool Road, Birmingham, are some of the examples that I have in mind here.